A *Faulkner*
Chronology

A Faulkner Chronology

by
MICHEL GRESSET

Translated from
Faulkner: Oeuvres Romanesques
by Arthur B. Scharff

Foreword by Noel Polk

University Press of Mississippi
JACKSON

This volume grew out of a project conceived and directed by Anne E. H. Freudenberg, assistant curator of manuscripts, in the Manuscripts Department of the University of Virginia Library to provide a reference tool for researchers in the Faulkner Collections there. It is excerpted from *Faulkner: Oeuvres Romanesques,* Vol. I, Editions Gallimard, 1977.

The University Press of Mississippi thanks Jill Faulkner Summers and Random House Inc., for permission to print excerpts from works by and about William Faulkner.

Library of Congress Cataloging in Publication Data

Gresset, Michel.
    A Faulkner chronology.

    "Excerpted from Faulkner: Oeuvres romanesques, vol. 1, Editions Gallimard, 1977"—T.p. verso.
    Includes bibliographical references and index.
    1. Faulkner, William, 1897–1962—Chronology.
2. Faulkner, William, 1897–1962—Biography. 3. Novelists, American—20th century—Biography. I. Title.
PS3511.A86Z78413   1985   813'.52 [B]   84-50873
ISBN 0-87805-229-1 (pbk.)

For Maurice Edgar Coindreau
il miglior fabbro

But in Oxford, Mississippi,
there lived a small, shy,
solitary man who was tormented
by dreams that he exorcised
by writing somber stories.[1]

It is my ambition to be, as a private individual, abolished and voided from history, leaving it markless, no refuse save the printed books; I wish I had had enough sense to see ahead thirty years ago and, like some of the Elizabethans, not signed them. It is my aim, and every effort bent, that the sum and history of my life, which in the same sentence is my obit and my epitaph too, shall be them both: He made the books and he died.

Faulkner to Malcolm Cowley
(11 February 1949)

---

[1]Maurice Edgar Coindreau, "William Faulkner and Ernest Hemingway," *Le Journal de Genève,* 13 December 1954; also in *TTWF,* p. 74.

Contents

Foreword

MICHEL GRESSET is one third of a galloping French troika that has helped to drag Faulkner studies, sometimes kicking and screaming, into the world of modern literary theoretical concerns. Through numerous essays in English and in French, on Faulkner and on others, and through his important book, *Faulkner ou la fascination* (Paris, 1982; to be published in English by Duke University Press), he has helped to show how the theoretical concerns of modern literary criticism can serve the study of Faulkner. He has established himself as among the premier critics of Faulkner writing in any language.

He is also, and not incidentally, the heir apparent to Maurice Edgar Coindreau's mantel as the preeminent translator of American literature; he has translated Faulkner's letters and is working on the *Uncollected Stories of William Faulkner*. In 1977 he completed years of work on the first volume of the Pléiade Faulkner, a magnificently-translated and -edited tome containing texts of *Sartoris, The Sound and the Fury, Sanctuary* and *As I Lay Dying*—translations by Coindreau and others corrected by Gresset, who, as early as 1965, had access to Faulkner's typescripts and manuscripts that the original translators did not have. For the volume he also translated the Compson Appendix as well as extensive passages from the original version of *Sanctuary* and from unpublished manuscript and typescript passages of *Flags in the Dust;* he added to the volume a full record of variants from typescripts and manuscripts, translated into French, thus providing to French readers much material that was and still is unavailable to Americans. Finally, he appended copious annotations for French readers, and an extensive and detailed chronology of Faulkner's life and career. All of which proves that Gresset is not just a graceful and witty critic, something of a poet himself (you have to be something of a poet to translate Faulkner), but also a hard-core scholar who is not afraid to own up to a passion for bibliographical exactitude.

The present volume is a translation of the Pléiade's Chronology, expanded and updated to account for scholarship done since 1977, including various biographical essays by Carvel Collins and Joseph Blotner, and Blotner's one-volume *Faulkner: A Biography* of 1984. The work chronicles not just Faulkner's life but also the essentials of his critical reception—the development of the Faulkner field—from the beginning to 1985, twenty-two years after his death. The log is, obviously, a highly eclectic and personal chronology, reflecting Gresset's own sense of what is important in Faulkner's life and career; some events he merely records, others are the occasions for speculation and extended comment.

It is a biographical skeleton extrapolated from published biographical studies, useful and usable in that it makes available at one glance the essential information about a given period in Faulkner's career, the bare facts of his life and work juxtaposed to each other and to events outside the life and work in ways which can expose the impulse at the source of a particular piece of work. To have ready to hand, for example, a list of the novels and stories Faulkner wrote and/or published during a given year or month so sharply juxtaposed to each other and to the record of his very complex relations with his publishers, agents, family, and friends, can be very revealing of the way his life, his character, and his work mesh.

The *Chronology* will not, of course, replace Blotner's work, or the more specialized biographical work of others; nor is it intended to, though I suspect many will come to rely on it as a handy quick-reference tool. It will be a very useful companion volume to them all, drawing, as it does, on them for its own substance, and referring the reader to them for fuller discussions. Those of us who have for years depended on our own home-made logs will welcome Gresset's volume, which has been deliberately designed to allow each user to add such details as are necessary to his own work. I am happy to have it available.

Noel Polk

Hattiesburg, Mississippi
January 1985

Preface

MY AMBITION in writing the following *Chronology* is to help the student study Faulkner's works as related to his life. This is not a biography, nor a biographical sketch, nor even a bibliography, except incidentally. Yet this *Chronology* has something of both: it could be described as a biobibliography, or perhaps even better as the outline of a literary career. It may be said to rest on the following assumptions.

It is highly doubtful whether such a rich and complex literary achievement as Faulkner's could be accounted for, let alone understood, without a sense of evolution, if not necessarily of progress. It is nevertheless quite clear now that repetition is and must be an integral part of any literary project; so, if the image of a straight line must be ruled out as a neopositivist illusion, that of a spiral made of several fragments, or vectors (r)evolving around an axis, can perhaps be used to describe Faulkner's literary career in spatial terms.

Time, however, must of course be the axis of such a chronology, not only for methodological considerations, but because, like all other human activities except dreams, writing takes time: it is even responsible for consuming the life of a man working, like Faulkner, in the "anguish and travail," "the agony and the sweat" of "the human heart in conflict with itself"—and with the world at large.

If the following "facts" (which have been carefully selected in order to avoid the pitfalls of pedantic scholarship and the mirages of interpretive hypotheses) amount to any, or to some, truth, it must be that Faulkner was certainly not without blemish as a man, but that, as a writer, he was an intense and hard-working craftsman, almost ruthless when it came to defending or protecting what was most precious to him against the meddling goodwill of publishers or the vulgarities and misunderstanding of the reading public.

The figure that looms behind this *Chronology* is that of a hard-gutted and hard-fisted little man whose rather unhappy life may well have found only in literature (and perhaps in his only daughter rather than in any of the women in his life) the deep satisfaction, at once physical and spiritual, like deep breathing, that he never ceased to yearn after.

In compiling this *Chronology*, I have given priority to the main events in the *writer*'s life, which includes as much of his professional activity as could be encompassed in the format: the inception, composition, revisions, if any, eventually the publication, and occasionally the republication or the reworking of the same material for other ends, of all of his major works, i.e., of all the books (the novels as well as the collections of poems and of short stories) and of all the prose pieces published individually during his lifetime, as well as some of the poems published separately, some of the essays, speeches, and public letters, and some of the film treatments and scripts.

As will be seen, each individual year after 1930 is followed by a complete, recapitulative list of the stories published during that year, and all the published works appear at least once, under the dates of their publication. The publication dates are also emphasized by page numbers in italics in the index, which is strictly limited to the names and titles mentioned in the *Chronology*.

For reasons implicit in the very idea and format of this *Chronology*, it has been impossible to list, even briefly, the main events of world history, or even American history, between 1897 and 1962. In order for the *Chronology* to remain a coherent and self-explanatory tool, everything had to be described, or seen, not through Faulkner's eyes, but in relation to him; this explains why I have sometimes alluded to local history and the history of Mississippi. Nor was it possible to weave the critical reception of his works (including the foreign reception) into the fabric of his life: too much material was involved and this has been the subject of several books.

In the twenty-three years that have elapsed since Faulkner's death in 1962, more and more primary materials have been made available through publication, mostly thanks to the liberal policy of his literary executrix, Mrs. Jill Faulkner Summers. I have used them as lavishly as possible, particularly Faulkner's own letters. Though I have emphasized his professional or public life, which obviously includes his travels and his trips to Hollywood, there are private aspects of his public life—often deeply moving and sometimes even pathetic—which I have chosen to bring to light, because in my opinion they belong in his life as a writer. On the other hand, I have not even tried to deal with Faulkner's family life, because I consider this the biographer's domain.

I must hasten to acknowledge my debt to Joseph Blotner, without whose monumental work this skeleton of Faulkner's career would probably not even exist, and who, I hope, will approve of my purpose, which is to provide the student of Faulkner's work with a handy tool to check it, as it were, against his life. It is obvious that his 1,846-page *Faulkner: A Biography* (or the 778-page one-volume version of it published last year), and even the 251-page interpretative biography by David Minter are quite different propositions.

My acknowledgments must also go to two other pioneers: Carvel Collins, for the invaluable factual information provided by his introductions to the early writings of William Faulkner, and James B. Meriwether, for the unequalled precision of the bibliographical wealth he has accumulated over the years. And finally, my thanks go both to Anne E. H. Freudenberg, Assistant Curator of Manuscripts at the Alderman Library of the University of Virginia, who was the first to see the value of this *Chronology*, and to Arthur B. Scharff who translated much of it from the original French version in *Faulkner: Oeuvres Romanesques* (Paris: Gallimard, 1977).

List of Abbreviations

AFM James B. Meriwether, ed. *A Faulkner Miscellany.* Jackson: University Press of Mississippi, 1974.

CSWF William Faulkner, *Collected Stories of William Faulkner.* New York: Random House, 1950.

DrM William Faulkner, *Doctor Martino and Other Stories.* New York: Harrison Smith and Robert Haas, 1934.

EPAP William Faulkner, *William Faulkner: Early Prose and Poetry,* ed. Carvel Collins. Boston and Toronto: Little, Brown, 1962.

ESPL William Faulkner, *Essays, Speeches & Public Letters,* ed. James B. Meriwether. New York: Random House, 1965.

FAB Joseph Blotner, *Faulkner: A Biography.* 2 vols. New York: Random House, 1974.

FACCE Robert Penn Warren, ed., *Faulkner: A Collection of Critical Essays.* Englewood Cliffs, New Jersey: Prentice-Hall, 1966.

FAF Bruce F. Kawin, *Faulkner and Film.* New York: Frederick Ungar, 1977.

FIH Joseph Blotner, "Faulkner in Hollywood" in *Man and the Movies,* ed. W. R. Robinson. Baton Rouge: Louisiana State University Press, 1969; reprinted by Pelican Books (Baltimore, 1969), pp. 261–303.

FITU Frederick L. Gwynn and Joseph L. Blotner, eds., *Faulkner in the University: Class Conferences at the University of Virginia 1957–1958.* Charlottesville: University Press of Virginia, 1959.

HAC William Faulkner, *Helen: A Courtship.* Introductory essays by Carvel Collins and Joseph Blotner. Oxford, Mississippi: Tulane University and Yoknapatawpha Press, 1981.

HLAW David Minter, *William Faulkner: His Life and Work.* Baltimore and London: Johns Hopkins University Press, 1980.

LCWF James B. Meriwether, *The Literary Career of William Faulkner*. Princeton: Princeton University Library, 1961. Second "authorized" edition, Columbia, South Carolina: University of South Carolina Press, 1971.

LITG William Faulkner, *Lion in the Garden: Interviews With William Faulkner, 1926–1962,* eds. James B. Meriwether and Michael Millgate. New York: Random House, 1968.

MBB John Faulkner, *My Brother Bill: An Affectionate Reminiscence.* New York: Trident Press, 1963.

NOS William Faulkner, *William Faulkner: New Orleans Sketches,* ed. Carvel Collins. Augmented version. New York: Random House, 1968.

SLWF William Faulkner, *Selected Letters of William Faulkner,* ed. Joseph Blotner. New York: Random House, 1977.

TAWF Michael Millgate, *The Achievement of William Faulkner.* New York: Random House, 1966.

TCH John Bassett, ed, *William Faulkner: The Critical Heritage.* London and Boston: Routledge & Kegan Paul, 1975.

TFCF Malcolm Cowley, ed. *The Faulkner-Cowley File: Letters and Memories, 1944–1962.* New York: Viking Press, 1966.

TFOM Murry Falkner, *The Falkners of Mississippi: A Memoir.* Baton Rouge: Louisiana State University Press, 1967.

T13 William Faulkner, *These 13.* New York: Jonathan Cape & Harrison Smith, 1931.

TTWF Maurice Edgar Coindreau, *The Time of William Faulkner: A French View of Modern American Fiction,* ed. and chief translator George McMillan Reeves. Columbia: University of South Carolina Press, 1971.

USWF William Faulkner, *Uncollected Stories of William Faulkner,* ed. Joseph Blotner. New York: Random House, 1979.

WFLAC Joseph Blotner, comp., *William Faulkner's Library: A Catalogue.* Charlottesville: University Press of Virginia, 1964.

A Faulkner
Chronology

A *Faulkner* *Chronology*

1540 Between 20,000 and 30,000 Indians, mostly Chickasaw, Choctaw, and Natchez, live in the present boundary of Mississippi. Hernando de Soto reaches the present site of Columbus; after his death in the vicinity of Natchez, the Spanish lose interest in the area.

1682 After Father Jacques Marquette, S. J., and trader Louis Jolliet explore the river as far south as the Arkansas River, Robert Cavelier de La Salle receives permission from King Louis XIV to explore the Mississippi River valley down to its mouth. They name the territory Louisiana.

1699 Pierre Lemoyne, Sieur d'Iberville, casts anchor off the coast of Mississippi and settles on Biloxi Bay.

1702 Mobile founded.

1716 Fort Rosalie (now Natchez) established.

1729 Open warfare between the French and the Natchez Indians and their allies, the Chickasaws.

1754–1763 The English win the "French and Indian War" and force the French to cede all of their territorial claims east of the river, except the site of New Orleans.

1798   Mississippi Territory (population 5,000) organized under U.S. Law, with Winthrop Sargent as first governor and Natchez as first capital.

1803   Louisiana Purchase.

1812   War with Mexico and Indian trouble. General Andrew Jackson is sent to restore order.

1814   *9 August*   By the treaty of Fort Jackson, the Indians are forced to cede their land to the federal government. The new territory is so large that it is divided into two states, Mississippi (1817) and Alabama (1819).

1817   *10 December*   Mississippi is admitted to the Union as the twentieth state.

1820   Missouri Compromise. Population of Mississippi is 75,448.

1825   *6 July*   William Clark Falkner (the novelist's great-grandfather), son of Joseph Falkner, an immigrant from Scotland, and of Caroline Word, is born in Tennessee.

1832   On behalf of the Chickasaws, King Ishtehotopah signs the Treaty of Pontotoc, which opens northern Mississippi to white settlers, among whom is Robert Shegog.[2]

1833   According to Faulkner, date of the "patent" for his future property, Rowanoak:[3] "a few Chickasaws still retained holdings under the white man's setup."[4]

---

[2] "'Colonel' Robert Shegog was an Irishman who left County Down during the first third of the nineteenth century to sail to America. He prospered in Tennessee, and by the time he moved to Mississippi he was a wealthy man" (*FAB*, p. 651).

[3] A "rowan" tree is a mountain ash. According to Blotner (*FAB*, pp. 660–61), Faulkner got this name from Frazer's *The Golden Bough*. Faulkner spelled the name inconsistently, as one or as two words (*FAB*, p. 668).

[4] Letter received by Malcolm Cowley on 7 November 1945; in *SLWF*, p. 208.

1834   *24 July*   John Wesley Thompson (William Clark Falkner's maternal uncle, born in 1809) marries Justiania Dickinson Word.

1836   Lafayette County, Mississippi, is created, bounded on the north by the Tallahatchie River and on the south by the Yocona (formerly Yoconapatafa) River. Oxford is soon after chosen as its county seat.

1840   William Clark Falkner arrives, on foot, according to the family legend, in Mississippi (first at Pontotoc, then at Ripley), where his uncle will play the role of a foster father or guardian to him.

1844   Robert Shegog acquires the tract of land on which he has an English architect build the house later to be known as Rowan Oak (see *12 April 1930*).

1847   *9 July*   After returning from the siege of Monterrey, where he was wounded, W. C. Falkner marries Holland Pearce in Knoxville, Tennessee.

1848   *2 September*   John Wesley Thompson Falkner (the novelist's grandfather), the only child of W. C. Falkner and Holland Pearce, is born in Ripley, Mississippi. The University of Mississippi opens; Augustus Longstreet (*Georgia Scenes,* 1835) is president (1849–1856).

1849   *Spring*   W. C. Falkner kills Robert Hindman.[5]
       31 May   Holland Pearce dies.

1850   *14 October*   Sallie McAlpine Murry (the novelist's paternal grandmother), the future wife of John W. T. Falkner, is born.

---

[5] "It was clear that Falkner had acted in self-defense and when the case eventually came to trial he was acquitted" (*FAB,* p. 16).

1851 *12 October* W. C. Falkner takes as his second wife Elizabeth ("Lizzie") Houston Vance. Between January 1853 and May 1874, they have eight children, four of whom die at an early age. *The Siege of Monterrey,* an autobiographical poem by W. C. Falkner, is published in Cincinnati, Ohio.

1860 Mississippi's population is 791,305. "Flush times are over." W. C. Falkner's fortune estimated at $50,000.

1861 *7 January* At the State Secession Convention, Lafayette County has two representatives: L. Q. C. Lamar and Dr. T. D. Isom; the latter is against secession.
May W. C. Falkner is elected colonel of the Magnolia Rifles, soon to participate valiantly in the battles of Manassas. In an important letter sent to Malcolm Cowley on 8 December 1945, William Faulkner writes: "My great-grandfather, whose name I bear, was a considerable figure in his time and provincial milieu. He was prototype of John Sartoris: raised, organized, paid the expenses of and commanded the 2nd Mississippi Infantry, 1861–2, etc. Was a part of Stonewall Jackson's left at 1st Manassas that afternoon; we have a citation in James Longstreet's longhand as his corps commander after 2nd Manassas" (*SLWF,* p. 211).

1862 General Grant occupies Oxford, Mississippi, without damaging it.

1863 Replaced as commander of his first regiment, Colonel Falkner forms another, the Partisan Rangers, and reenters the war.

1864 *9 August* General Andrew J. Smith burns the Oxford town square.

1869 *2 September* J. W. T. Falkner marries Sallie McAlpine Murry and settles in Ripley, Mississippi.

1870 *17 August* Murry Cuthbert Falkner (the novelist's father), first child of J. W. T. Falkner and Sallie Murry, is born. In

1958, Faulkner would say: "From '70 on to 1912–14, nothing happened to Americans to speak of."[6]

1871 Reconstruction of the Oxford courthouse and jail is begun. A charter for the Ripley Railroad Company is issued to W. C. Falkner and others (Falkner will later become its president).
27 November Maud Butler (the novelist's mother), daughter of Charles Butler and of Lelia (Leila according to David Minter)[7] Dean Swift ("Damuddy") is born.

1872 *16 December* Mary Holland ("Auntee"), second child of J. W. T. Falkner and Sallie Murry, is born.

1874 *7 May* Alabama LeRoy ("Aunt Bama"), eighth and last child of W. C. Falkner and Lizzie Vance, is born.

1881 *June* Publication in book form of W. C. Falkner's novel, *The White Rose of Memphis,* previously serialized in the Ripley *Advertiser.* By 1909, the book had been reprinted 35 times and had sold more than 160,000 copies.[8]

1882 *25 July* J. W. T. Falkner, Jr. ("Uncle John"), third and last child of J. W. T. Falkner and Sallie Murry, is born. He grew to become a respected lawyer and judge in Oxford. W. C. Falkner's *The Little Brick Church,* a reply to *Uncle Tom's Cabin,* is published (1852).[9]

1884 W. C. Falkner's *Rapid Ramblings in Europe* is published.

1885 J. W. T. Falkner moves from Ripley to Oxford.

---

[6] See *FITU,* p. 251.

[7] See *HLAW,* pp. 10, 256.

[8] Robert Cantwell, "Introduction," *The White Rose of Memphis,* by Col. William C. Falkner (New York: Coley Taylor, 1953), p. v.

[9] The novel is called *Lady Olivia* in an abridged edition. See Cantwell, "Introduction," *The White Rose of Memphis,* p. xxiv.

7

1888   Inauguration of the Middleton, Tennessee–Pontotoc, Mississippi Railroad (the "Falkner Railroad").

1889   *6 November*   W. C. Falkner, wounded the day before by Richard Jackson Thurmond, a former associate who had become his rival in business and defeated him in a race for the state legislature, dies in Ripley, where his statue can still be seen.

1895   *15 November*   J. W. T. Falkner is elected to the Senate of the state of Mississippi.

1896   *19 February*   Lida Estelle Oldham, daughter of Judge Lemuel Earl Oldham and Lida Allen, and the future wife of the novelist in a second marriage, is born.
8 November   Murry C. Falkner and Maud Butler announce they have just been married.[10] They settle in New Albany.

* * *

1897   *25 September*   William Cuthbert Falkner, the first of the four sons of Murry C. Falkner and Maud Butler, is born on Jefferson Street, New Albany, Union County, Mississippi. His father is employed in the administration of the railroad built by his grandfather.

1898   Murry C. Falkner is appointed treasurer of the railroad company and moves to Ripley.

1899   *14 June*   Sallie Murry Wilkins, daughter of James P. Wilkins and Mary Holland Falkner, is born. After the death of her father in 1904, this cousin will be reared in the Falkner home: "Throughout our childhood Sallie Murry and Bill and John and

---

[10] 8 November 1896 was a Sunday. Joseph Blotner writes: "It was actually a Saturday on which the marriage took place" (*FAB*, p. 31). However, David Minter dates it 9 November in *HLAW*, p. 256.

I could not have been any closer had we been sister and brothers," Murry Faulkner writes in his memoir of his family.[11]

26 June Murry Charles, Jr. ("Jack"), second son of Murry C. Falkner and Maud Butler, is born in Ripley.

1900 According to the census, Mississippi ranks twentieth out of the forty-eight states with a population of 1,551,270. The population of Jackson, the capital, is 7,816 (compared with which Memphis, Tennessee, has a population of 102,320) and of Oxford 1,825.[12]

1901 *24 September* John Wesley Thompson III ("Johncy"), third son of Murry C. Falkner and Maud Butler, is born. He was to become a regional novelist and write an "affectionate reminiscence" of his "brother Bill."[13]

1902 *Autumn* Sale of the family railroad for $75,000. Murry C. Falkner moves with his wife, children, and Caroline Barr, the black nurse, to "The Big Place" in Oxford, where they are joined by Lelia Butler, his mother-in-law. After several other business ventures, all more or less unsuccessful, he operates a livery stable. In a letter to Malcolm Cowley, Faulkner writes: "I more or less grew up in my father's livery stable. Being the eldest of four boys, I escaped my mother's influence pretty easy, since my father thought it was fine for me to apprentice to the business. I imagine I would have been in the livery stable yet if it hadn't been for motor car" (*SLWF*, p. 212).

1905 *25 September* William Falkner enters school in first grade. According to Murry C. Falkner, reading in the family consisted of James Fenimore Cooper's tales of the American Indians, Dickens, *Treasure Island, Robinson Crusoe,* Grimm's

---

[11] See *TFOM*, p. 7.

[12] By the time Faulkner died in 1962, the city population had tripled.

[13] John Faulkner, *My Brother Bill: An Affectionate Reminiscence* (New York: Trident Press, 1963).

Fairy Tales, Joel Chandler Harris's *Uncle Remus,* Mark Twain, Owen Wister's *The Virginian,* and various books on the War between the States. Later came Kipling, Poe, Conrad, Cabell, Shakespeare, Balzac, and Hugo (*TFOM,* p. 17).

1906   *21 December*   Sallie Murry Falkner dies.[14]

1907   A monument to the county's Civil War heroes is erected on the town square in Oxford.
1 June   Lelia Dean Swift Butler dies.
15 August   Dean Swift Falkner, fourth and last child of Murry C. Falkner and Maud Butler, is born.

1910   *4 October*   J. W. T. Falkner establishes the First National Bank of Oxford with capital of $30,000.

1914   *Summer*   William Falkner, who has begun to write poetry and is about to quit school, becomes acquainted with Phil Stone, the son of "General"[15] James Stone, a lawyer and a banker like J. W. T. Falkner. Four years his senior, the future lawyer and lover of *belles lettres* soon plays the part of mentor to the young writer at the beginning of his career. According to Stone, he was the one who made Faulkner read "Swinburne, Keats and a number of the then moderns, such as Conrad Aiken and the Imagists in verse and Sherwood Anderson and the others in prose" (*FAB,* p. 164).

1915   *19 March*   The local newspaper mentions William Falkner as one of the guests at a masked ball at the home of "Major" and Mrs. Oldham, whose daughter Estelle was then both the inspirer and recipient of the young man's early poems.

---

[14] The date "21 February" which is given in the genealogical tables of both *FAB* and *SLWF* is an error: Sallie Murry died "four days before Christmas" (*FAB,* 105).

[15] Often in the South after the Civil War, prominent men were given military titles which had not necessarily been won in combat. Thus was the case with the son of the "Old Colonel," who was called the "Young Colonel," and with R. J. Cofield, who took many photographs of Faulkner and whom everyone knew as the "Colonel."

1915–16 In November 1953, Faulkner writes: "Because I hadn't thought of writing books then. The future didn't extend so far. I had seen an aeroplane and my mind was filled with names: Ball, Immelman and Boelcke, and Guynemer and Bishop, and I was waiting, biding, until I would be old enough or free enough or anyway could get to France and become glorious and beribboned too."[16]

1916 William Falkner works temporarily as an assistant book-keeper at his grandfather's bank, but he is more interested in the student activities at the University of Mississippi, where he gets to know Ben Wasson (born 1900), who would become his first literary agent (see *27 February 1928*).
31 March The Oxford *Independent* publishes a map in which the road from Clarksdale to Corinth by way of Oxford, New Albany, and Ripley is called the "W. C. Falkner Highway"— but the local newspapers that year mention the name Oldham more frequently than the name Falkner. The latter, according to John W. T. Faulkner, III, were "not poor folks. It was simply that you did not waste" (*MBB*, p. 82). And about Faulkner's father, Blotner says: "He certainly did not measure up, in terms of this world's standards, to such men as Colonel Falkner, General Stone, and Major Oldham" (*FAB*, p. 221).

1917 Volume XXI of *Ole Miss,* the annual of the University of Mississippi, publishes the novelist's first known work, a draw-ing, signed "William Falkner."[17]
9 April Headline in the *Independent* reads: "War has been declared. America's sweet liberty is at stake."
22 October The same local newspaper publishes a list of French military terms "for those who are going away."

1918 *Spring* After having tried in vain to enlist in the air corps (according to Blotner [*FAB*, pp. 196, 211], his short stature—

---

[16] William Faulkner, "Foreword," *The Faulkner Reader* (New York: Random House, 1954), pp. ix–x.
[17] This drawing, as well as those which followed it, is reproduced in *EPAP*, p. 36.

5' 5½"—and lack of weight were the reasons he was turned down), Falkner goes to New Haven, Connecticut, where Phil Stone is reenrolled for a second degree at Yale. According to his brother John (*MBB,* p. 134), Falkner's visit may have been prompted by the engagement of Estelle Oldham to Cornell Franklin, at that time a lawyer in Hawaii.

10 April Falkner begins to work in the accounting office of the Winchester Repeating Arms Company under the name "Faulkner" (*EPAP,* p. 11).

18 April Estelle Oldham marries Cornell Franklin, whom she follows to Honolulu by the first of June.

May Murry Falkner enlists in the Marine Corps.

14 June In New York, Faulkner has an interview with representatives of the Royal Air Force (created on 1 April).

15 June He resigns his job as ledger clerk in New Haven.

9 July After a brief visit with his parents in Oxford, Faulkner arrives in Toronto to begin his ground training as a cadet (matriculation number 172799).

August While William is learning the Morse code, Murry lands at Brest (he was wounded in the Argonne on 1 November).

22 November At the end of a flight, Faulkner has to be "helped out of the cockpit." Had he been wounded? Blotner doubts it, even asking "Did he ever fly?" (*FAB,* pp. 223–26). On 1 February 1946, Faulkner nonetheless writes to Cowley: "The mishap was caused not by combat but by (euphoneously [sic]) 'cockpit trouble'; i.e. my own foolishness; the injury I suffered I still feel I got at bargain rates" (*SLWF,* p. 219).

1 December Murry C. Falkner is appointed assistant secretary at the University of Mississippi, a post (and a residence) he was to hold until June, 1930. Several days later, after 179 days in the R. A. F., his son William, deprived of his war by the Armistice of November, is back at home.[18]

1919–20 In his December 1945 letter to Cowley, Faulkner writes:

---

[18] ". . . they had stopped the war on him" is the authorial comment on Cadet Howe to be found on the first page of Faulkner's first novel, *Soldiers' Pay.*

"When I came back from RAF, my father's health was beginning to fail and he had a political job: business manager of the state University, given to him by a countryman whom my grandfather had made a lawyer of, who became governor of Mississippi. I didn't want to go to work; it was by my father's request that I entered the University, which I didn't want to do either. That was 1920 . . . [I] attended 1 year at the University of Mississippi by special dispensation for returned troops, studying European languages, still didn't like school and quit that. Rest of education undirected reading [see *1905* and *1922*]" (*SLWF*, p. 212).

1919 *4 January* Cadet William Faulkner receives his notice of discharge.

8 February Victoria Franklin ("Cho-Cho"), first child of Cornell Franklin and Estelle Oldham, is born.

March Return of Murry, Faulkner's younger brother.

Spring Faulkner writes the poems later to be collected as *The Marble Faun* (see *15 December 1924*).

6 August The first literary work signed "William Faulkner"[19] is published in *The New Republic,* a forty-line poem with a French title acknowledging the influence of the French Symbolists: "L'Apres-Midi d'un Faune" [sic] (*EPAP*, pp. 39–40).

19 September Faulkner enrolls at the University of Mississippi as a "special student" in the following courses: French, Spanish, second-year English literature.

November–December In the student newspaper, *The Mississippian,* appear successively, on *12 November,* a poem entitled "Cathay" (*EPAP*, p. 41); on *26 November,* "Landing in Luck," a nine-page short story or prose sketch of an anecdotal character (a flying accident), and "Sapphics," a poem (*EPAP*, pp. 42–52); and on *10 December,* "After Fifty Years," a poem (*EPAP*, p.

---

[19] "The answer to the question 'Who Put the "u" in William Faulkner's Name?' is William Faulkner" (*EPAP*, p. 13). It seems therefore that on becoming a writer Faulkner chose to distinguish himself from his family. Even though he was "Faulkner" in Toronto (see *8 July 1918*), he remained "William C. Falkner" to his great-aunt, Mrs. Alabama Falkner McLean (see *September 1925*); at the same time, he was "Billy" to his mother.

53). However, there is no doubt that Faulkner wrote many more poems than he could or would publish; some he used much later in his second and last published collection (see *20 April 1933*), others have remained unpublished until quite recently or even to this day.[20]

1920   *1 January*   Faulkner signs and dates "a small . . . beautifully produced booklet of poems, handlettered as a gift to a friend, titled *The Lilacs*" (*EPAP*,p. 11).

13 January   John W. T. Falkner is forced to resign as president of his bank by a *nouveau riche* named Joe Parks, who takes his place.[21]

January–April   After "Une Ballade des Femmes Perdues" (again in French, this time after Villon) and "Naiads' Song," Faulkner publishes four adaptations (rather than translations) from Paul Verlaine in *The Mississippian* (*EPAP*, pp. 54–61).

9 March   The London *Gazette* announces the promotion of William Faulkner to the rank of Honorary 2nd Lieutenant to take effect the date of his demobilization (*FAB*, p. 289).

24 March   The first known reaction to a piece written by Faulkner, a hostile comment, appears in *The Mississippian* (see reproduction in *EPAP*, pp. 13–14). An argument follows. It is clear that the young Faulkner, at the time, was wavering between bohemianism and dandyism, which was no more appreciated by the extremely provincial society in which he lived than the "decadent" poetry which he produced.

June   A small prize for poetry is awarded to Faulkner by Calvin S. Brown, a professor at the University of Mississippi.

Summer   Faulkner works as house-painter in Oxford.

Autumn   Again enrolled as a special student in the university, Faulkner, along with Ben Wasson and Lucy Somerville, participates in the founding of a dramatic club called "The Marionettes," for which he writes a one-act play in the manner

---

[20] See Keen Butterworth, "A Census of Manuscripts and Typescripts of William Faulkner's Poetry" in *AFM*, pp. 70–97.

[21] "By now Joe Parks was one of the most prosperous men in the community, and his figure, with its bow tie, was a familiar one." In this description by Blotner (*FAB*, p. 258), the allusion to Flem Snopes appears unmistakable.

of the Symbolists, with the same title, *The Marionettes*,[22] which was never staged.

5 November   Faulkner drops out of the university. He begins to publish book reviews in *The Mississippian*.

10 November   The first review is devoted to William A. Percy, a poet who, "like alas! how many of us—suffered the misfortune of having been born out of his time" (*EPAP*, p. 71).

1921   *7 January*   Performance of a three-act farce, *The Arrival of Kitty*, by the Marionettes.

16 February   Faulkner writes an article favoring the poetry of Conrad Aiken, "in the fog generated by the mental puberty of contemporary American versifiers . . . one rift of heaven sent blue . . ." (EPAP, p. 74).

Summer   Faulkner completes an eighty-eight-page collection of love poems entitled *Vision in Spring*, meant as a token of his love for Estelle Franklin, and gives it to her during one of her visits to her parents.[23]

Autumn   At the suggestion of Stark Young,[24] Faulkner takes up a job in New York, as assistant in a bookstore managed by Elizabeth Prall, the future Mrs. Sherwood Anderson.

10 December   Upon his return to Oxford, Faulkner takes an examination for fourth-class postmaster at the university, a job lasting from the spring of 1922 to 31 October 1924. The annual salary of $1,500 enables him to buy a Ford, which he paints yellow.

1922   *13 January*   Faulkner reviews a one-act play by Edna St. Vincent Millay, *Aria da Capo*, in *The Mississippian* (*EPAP*, pp. 84–85).

3 February   Writes a favorable article on the "healthy" plays of Eugene O'Neill (*EPAP*, pp. 86–89).

---

[22] William Faulkner, *The Marionettes*, ed. Noel Polk (Charlottesville: University Press of Virginia, 1977). This is a facsimile edition of one of the four surviving manuscript copies of the play, the "Virginia" copy.

[23] William Faulkner, *Vision in Spring*, ed. Judith L. Sensibar (Austin: University of Texas Press, 1984).

[24] The best-known novel of this Mississippi-born writer (1881–1963) is probably *So Red the Rose* (1934).

10 March Publication in *The Mississippian* of "The Hill," a short prose poem of great importance to the author's future work. Without naming them yet, he uses here, for the first time, the rural setting of his future Yoknapatawpha novels and produces his first objective or "real life" character, "the tieless casual" (*EPAP,* pp. 90–92).

13 March John W. T. Falkner, the novelist's grandfather, "the loneliest man I've ever known," according to John Faulkner (*MBB,* p. 73), dies.

17 and 24 March Two articles on "American Drama: Inhibitions" published in *The Mississippian,* the first of which takes Freud to task, while the second extols America's two inexhaustible "fund[s] of dramatic material": "the old Mississippi river days, and the romantic growth of railroads" (*EPAP,* pp. 93–97).

April 12 First of nineteen issues of *The Fugitive* published in Nashville, Tennessee, by a group of Vanderbilt University poets and critics calling themselves "The Fugitives."

June "Portrait," a poem, published in the newly founded New Orleans literary magazine, *The Double Dealer.*

15 December Publication in *The Mississippian* of a severely critical review of three novels by Joseph Hergesheimer, quite a successful writer of the time (*EPAP,* pp. 101–03).

Orders from Phil Stone to a bookstore in New Haven, Connecticut, are dated in various months of 1922. That Faulkner read some, if not all, of these books is shown by the fact that most of the titles he reviewed the same year are among them. The list includes the names of Henry Adams, Conrad Aiken, Willa Cather, Catullus, Havelock Ellis, Euripides, Elie Faure, Edna Ferber, F. Scott Fitzgerald, Anatole France, Hilda Doolittle, Percy Lubbock *(The Craft of Fiction),* Edgar Lee Masters, Melville *(Moby Dick;* see *16 July 1927),* H. L. Mencken, Eugene O'Neill, Plato, Sophocles, Swinburne, W. C. Williams, and Elinor Wylie, as well as books of psychology and even physiology.[25]

---

[25] See "Appendix: Book Purchases and Orders by Phil Stone" in *WFLAC,* pp. 123–27.

1923 *20 June–23 November* Correspondence between Faulkner and the Four Seas Company, a publisher in Boston, concerning the publication of a manuscript entitled "Orpheus and Other Poems." Since publication proves impossible without a financial contribution which the author is unable to provide, the manuscript is returned to him (*FAB,* pp. 347–50). Faulkner nonetheless continues to write poems as well as his very first short stories, the earliest of which are apparently "Adolescence," "Love," and "Moonlight." These can hardly be called remarkable except by a historian of the novelist's literary creation.[26] Meanwhile, in the university yearbook, one finds that "Count Falkner" is awarded the honor, ironically, of being the hardest worker (as postmaster) for the year 1923.

3 December Malcolm Argyle Franklin ("Mac"), second and last child of Estelle Oldham by Cornell Franklin, is born.

1924 *13 May* Phil Stone writes to the Four Seas Company to offer the manuscript of *The Marble Faun,* which is accepted.

August Faulkner is now the master of the local boy scout troop. At the end of his letter (8 December 1945) to Malcolm Cowley, he writes: "Oh yes, was a scoutmaster for two years, was fired for moral reasons." Cowley adds: "That is, because he was the author of *Sanctuary*"[27]—which is impossible, considering the dates. Drinking was probably, and already, the issue.

September In a telegram to the Boston publisher, Phil Stone writes: "Faulkner tells me to authorize you to use any facts real or imaginary that you desire to use in the book [*The Marble Faun*] or advertising matter."[28] His words to Stone are a good

---

[26] It was James B. Meriwether who first reported the existence of these unpublished stories in *LCWF,* pp. 86–88. They were also listed in *William Faulkner: "Man Working," 1919–1962: A Catalogue of the William Faulkner Collections at the University of Virginia,* comp. Linton R. Massey (Charlottesville: University Press of Virginia, 1968), p. 229, and in *Man Collecting the Works of William Faulkner* (Charlottesville: University Printing Office, 1975), p. 135. For an explanation of James B. Meriwether's role, see *10 May–30 August 1957.*

[27] See *TFCF,* p. 68n. As all of Faulkner's letters published in this collection were also published in 1977 in Joseph Blotner's *Selected Letters,* it is used here only to highlight Cowley's own letters and comments.

[28] Quoted by James B. Meriwether and Michael Millgate in *LITG,* p. x.

example of the attitude of Faulkner toward biography; however, he did write for the publisher a short biographical sketch which has nothing imaginary about it: "Born in Mississippi in 1897. Great-grandson of Col. W. C. Faulkner [sic], C. S. A., author of *The White Rose of Memphis, Rapid Ramblings in Europe,* etc. Boyhood and youth were spent in Mississippi, since then has been (1) undergraduate (2) house painter (3) tramp, day laborer, dishwasher in various New England cities (4) clerk in Lord and Taylor's book shop in New York City (5) bank- and postal clerk. Served during the war in the British Royal Air Force. A member of Sigma Alpha Epsilon Fraternity. Present temporary address, Oxford, Miss. *The Marble Faun* was written in the spring of 1919" (*SLWF,* p. 7).

16 October   Faulkner signs and dates in Oxford one version of the last poem, then entitled "Mississippi Hills: My Epitaph," from his second collection, *A Green Bough* (1933).

November   Faulkner is in New Orleans, where he meets Sherwood Anderson, who has recently married Elizabeth Prall (see *Autumn 1921*).

15 December   Publication of *The Marble Faun,* in an edition of 1,000 copies, by the Four Seas Company in Boston. Dedicated to his mother, the book has a preface by Phil Stone.

16 December   A short paragraph published in the New Orleans *Times-Picayune* notes that William Faulkner is supposed to be "preparing to leave . . . for England and Italy."[29] The trip was to be delayed.

20 December   Date of Faulkner's first known Last Will and Testament.

25 December: Faulkner spends Christmas at home with his family.

1925   *4 January*   Accompanied by Phil Stone, Faulkner is back in New Orleans, where he lives within an active and lively circle of writers and artists centered around the young literary magazine *The Double Dealer,* whose offices are at 204 Baronne

---

[29] Quoted by Carvel Collins in "Faulkner at the University of Mississippi" (*EPAP,* p. 31).

Street, and in which were published the first works of Hart Crane, Ernest Hemingway, Robert Penn Warren, and Edmund Wilson. His neighbor at 624 Orleans Alley is a young painter, William Spratling.[30]

January–February Number 41–42 of volume 7 of *The Double Dealer* contains the following work by Faulkner: an essay entitled "On Criticism," in which the author regrets that American critics are more interested in the writers than in their works (*EPAP*, pp. 109–12); a poem entitled "Dying Gladiator" (*EPAP*, p. 113); the announcement of a collection of poems to be entitled "A Greening Bough"; and eleven short descriptive sketches of life in the city entitled "New Orleans" (*NOS*, pp. 3–14).[31]

8 February While Faulkner is reported to be at work on his first novel, the *Times-Picayune* begins the publication of sixteen texts, or short stories, the last of which appears on 27 September. Some of these, such as "The Kingdom of God," which adumbrates the character of Benjy Compson, are extremely interesting.[32]

3 March After a short stay in Oxford, Faulkner returns to New Orleans.

April Number 43 of volume 3 of *The Double Dealer* contains, in addition to a poem entitled "The Faun," dedicated "To H. L." (Harold Levy, a musically talented friend, who helped him finish the sonnet [*FAB*, pp. 420–21]), an extremely important article "Verse Old and Nascent: A Pilgrimage" (*EPAP*, pp. 114–19), in which the poet retraces with great lucidity the path that led him from Swinburne, a youthful error, to Housman and Keats, the poet *par excellence,* through Shelley and

---

[30] See Chapter 3, "New Orleans, 1922–1929," in William Spratling, *File on Spratling* (Boston: Little, Brown, 1967).

[31] These sketches were republished by Carvel Collins in *William Faulkner: New Orleans Sketches* (New Brunswick, New Jersey: Rutgers University Press, 1958; new edition with the addition of the essay on "Sherwood Anderson" of *26 April 1925,* New York: Random House, 1968). The abbreviation *NOS* used hereafter refers to the augmented, 1968 edition.

[32] Particularly the final vision of the idiot's "loud sorrow" and "ineffable blue eyes . . . dreaming above his narcissus clenched tightly in his dirty hands" (*NOS*, p. 60).

D. H. Lawrence, who "tortured sex." In April, too, *The Dial* (volume 77) publishes a story by Sherwood Anderson entitled "A Meeting South" in which Faulkner figures under the name of David, a young poet, small and frail, who limps and drinks, and whom the author takes to "Aunt Sally's"—actually "Aunt" Rose Arnold, a local madame (see *FAB*, pp. 370–71).

4 April The New Orleans *Item* runs a photograph of "William Faulkner, poet, philosopher and student of life" under the title "What is the Matter with Marriage?" "Nothing," the writer says, the problem is with "the people who entered into it and without being prepared to give and to understand" (*FAB*, p. 411). Faulkner wins ten dollars for answering the question in fewer than two hundred-fifty words.

26 April In a series called "Prophets of the New Age," the Dallas *Morning News* publishes a homage to Sherwood Anderson by Faulkner in the form of a short and very judicious comment on seven of his books, including *Winesburg, Ohio* (1919) (*NOS*, pp. 132–39).

May In New Orleans, Faulkner completes the typescript of *Soldiers' Pay* (the original title of which was Mayday [see *FAB*, ch. 23, and *SLWF*, p. 68]), which he sends, on the recommendation of Sherwood Anderson, to the publisher Horace Liveright.

June Faulkner spends some time at the Gulf Coast town of Pascagoula, Mississippi, at Phil Stone's brother's place. There he composes and dates the first seven poems of a small cycle which he would work on during his trip to Europe and complete in Oxford in June 1926, entitling it *Helen: A Courtship*. This Helen, to whom *Mosquitoes* is also dedicated, is Helen Baird, a fact substantiated by a handwritten love letter on the back of page 206 of the typescript of this novel.

7 July With a $200 advance on *Soldiers' Pay* from Liveright, Faulkner sails with William Spratling from New Orleans on board the freighter *West Ivis*.

11–14 July The *West Ivis* puts into port at Savannah, Georgia, where Faulkner probably sends off the last four sketches of the *Times-Picayune* series. The Scopes trial occurs at Dayton, Tennessee.

26 July The thirteenth sketch (the first to appear since 31

May), entitled "The Liar," establishes the setting and the type of rural characters later to become famous, especially in *The Hamlet* (1940).

2 August   The *West Ivis* drops anchor in Genoa, Italy.

6 August–15 October   Between these two dates Faulkner sends no fewer than twenty-five letters and postcards, all signed "Billy," to his mother, Mrs. Murry C. Falkner (see *SLWF,* pp. 8–31).

August   Still working on his poems to Helen, Faulkner visits Rapallo, Pavia, Milan, Stresa, and the small village of Sommariva, near Lake Maggiore, where he lives with the peasants—as he writes to his great-aunt "Bama" McLean in September[33]—then Switzerland (which he does not like), and finally France, where he arrives on 12 August. ". . . France, poor beautiful unhappy France. So innately kind, despite their racial lack of natural courtesy, so palpably keeping a stiff upper lip, with long lists of names in all the churches no matter how small, and having to fight again in Maroc" (*SLWF,* p. 19).

18 August   Faulkner moves from Montparnasse to 26 rue Servandoni—a stone's throw from the Senate and the Luxembourg Gardens.

26 August   Sherwood Anderson writes to his publisher, Horace Liveright: "I am glad you are going to publish Faulkner's novel [*Soldiers' Pay*]. I have a hunch this man is a comer. I'll tell you a lot about him when I see you in late October or November."[34]

September   In a letter to Aunt Bama, Faulkner writes: "I live just around the corner from the Luxembourg Gardens, where I spend all my time. I write there, and play with the children, help them sail their boats, etc. There is an old bent man who sails a toy boat on the pool, with the most beautiful rapt face you ever saw. When I am old enough to no longer have to make excuses for not working, I shall have a weathered derby hat like his and spend my days sailing a toy boat in the Luxembourg Gardens" (*SLWF,* pp. 19–20).

This letter, signed "William C. Falkner," is followed by a

---

[33] See 7 *May* 1874.

[34] Howard M. Jones and Walter B. Rideout, eds., *The Letters of Sherwood Anderson* (Boston: Little, Brown), p. 146.

postscript: "I have a beard, like this"—under which is drawn a faun-like self-portrait.[35]

6 September Faulkner writes to his mother: "I have just written such a beautiful thing that I am about to bust—2,000 words about the Luxembourg gardens and death. It has a thin thread of plot, about a young woman, and it is poetry though written in prose form."[36]

In Paris, Faulkner also works on a novel, *Elmer,* which he never finished and which exists in several versions.[37] On 12 March 1958, he told James B. Meriwether that it was "funny, but not funny enough"[38]—and one can only agree that he was right. *Elmer* is about an American who has come to Paris in order to learn the sensuous art of painting. In the company of a young Italian friend, Angelo, he is seated at the terrace of a café in Montparnasse where, whether through dialogue or through a faintly Joycean stream of consciousness, he reveals aspects of a past of which certain episodes are interesting. The unfinished whole, however, made up of anecdotes badly tied together, is uneven, and in spite of a conspicuous effort to that effect, the narrative lacks a sense of the author's distance from material that is barely transposed from autobiography.[39]

Did Faulkner meet Joyce? Questioned on the subject on 13 March 1957, he replied: "I knew of Joyce, and I would go to some effort to go to the café that he inhabited to look at him. But that was the only literary man that I remember seeing in Europe in those days" (*FITU,* p. 58).

---

[35] Reproduced in several places in *Man Collecting: The Works of William Faulkner.*

[36] Compare with the 350 words of the final scene of *Sanctuary.*

[37] The longer one, an unfinished and incomplete 136–page typescript simply entitled *Elmer,* was first published by *The Mississippi Quarterly,* 36 (Summer 1983) 343–447, then in a limited edition of 226 copies by the Seajay Press of Northport, Alabama (1983). A much more satisfactory version was the long short story Faulkner drew out of the Elmer material in 1935 but which was not published until 1979 in *USWF,* pp. 610–41.

[38] Quoted by James B. Meriwether in *LCWF,* p. 81, and in his foreword to *Elmer,* p. 340 (*The Mississippi Quarterly* edition).

[39] Even the fact that Elmer wants to be a painter and not a writer is hardly a transposition, since in 1925 Faulkner was still very much interested in painting. See Thomas McHaney, "The Elmer Papers: Faulkner's Comic Portrait of the Artist," in *AFM,* pp. 37–69.

22 September   On the day he travels from Rennes to Rouen (*FAB*, p. 467), a letter to his mother (whose hobby was painting) is postmarked in Paris: "I have spent afternoon after afternoon in the Louvre. . . . I have seen Rodin's museum, and 2 private collections of Matisse and Picasso (who are yet alive and painting) as well as numberless young and struggling moderns. And Cézanne! That man dipped his brush in light like Tobe Caruthers would dip his in red lead to paint a lamppost" (*SLWF*, p. 24).

6 October   After visiting Amiens (on 25 September, his twenty-eighth birthday) and Compiègne, from where he sends his mother a postcard showing the crossroads of the Armistice inaugurated at Rethondes on 11 November 1922, Faulkner embarks at Dieppe for Newhaven. He stays only a week in England, whereas he had planned to stay a month.

6 November   Phil Stone writes to the publisher of *The Marble Faun* for some money to assist Faulkner in Europe.

9 December   After returning from England as early as 15 October because "England was too dear for me" (*SLWF*, p. 31), Faulkner leaves from Cherbourg on board the *S.S. Republic*, bound for New York.

19 December   The ship drops anchor at Hoboken, New Jersey.

25 December   At home again, after "nearly half a *Wanderjahr* in Europe" (*FAB*, p. 483).

1926   *27 January*   Date on the manuscript of *Mayday*, a short allegorical piece dedicated to Helen Baird, and a work whose hero has more than one trait in common with Quentin Compson of *The Sound and the Fury*.[40]

25 February   At the time of the publication of *Soldiers' Pay*

---

[40] Although the title is the same as the one he had planned for *Soldiers' Pay*, the story has little to do with the novel. Here is how Carvel Collins, who edited *Mayday* (University of Notre Dame Press, 1978), summarized the story years earlier in his introduction to the *New Orleans Sketches*: "When Sir Galwyn of Arthgyl, rid of Hunger, the companion who has been on his right hand, and of Pain, the companion who has been on his left hand, approaches his end at the stream, he sees Saint Francis and gladly joins the shining maiden who he learns is Little Sister Death" (*NOS*, p. xxx).

by Boni and Liveright in New York, in an edition of 2,500 copies, Faulkner is back in New Orleans, where he resumes his pleasant association with Sherwood Anderson, William Spratling, and the other "Famous Creoles" (see *December 1926*).

29 April   In a letter to Horace Liveright, Sherwood Anderson complains about Faulkner's attitude toward him: "He was so nasty to me personally that I don't want to write him myself, but would be glad if you were to do it in this indirect way, as I surely think he is a good prospect."[41]

June   Faulkner completes and dates his collection of poems to Helen Baird. Having abandoned *Elmer,* he starts on his second novel, at that time called *Mosquito*. Meanwhile, in his first known interview, he claims to have worked "in a lumber mill . . . then on fishing boats . . ." (*LITG,* pp. 3–4).

1 September   In Pascagoula, Faulkner completes and dates the typescript of *Mosquitoes,* which he dedicates "To Helen, beautiful and wise." Then he returns to Oxford before going back to New Orleans.

29 October   Faulkner dedicates "To Estelle, a Lady with Respectful Admiration" a manuscript, hand-bound version, entitled *Royal Street,* of the "New Orleans Sketches" (see *January–February 1925*).

December   Publication of *Sherwood Anderson and Other Famous Creoles,* a collection of sketches and caricatures by William Spratling, with a foreword by William Faulkner that is rather inoffensive but that seems to have roused or heightened the annoyance of Anderson, whose style Faulkner parodies. The last paragraph of the foreword reads: "We have one priceless universal trait, we Americans. That trait is our humor. What a pity it is that it is not more prevalent in our art. This characteristic alone, being national and indigenous, could, by concentrating our emotional forces inward upon themselves, do for us what England's insularity did for English art during the reign of Elizabeth. Our trouble with us American artists is that we take our art and ourselves too seriously. And perhaps seeing ourselves in the eyes of our fellow artists, will enable those who

---

[41] *The Letters of Sherwood Anderson,* p. 155.

have strayed to establish anew a sound contact with the foun-tain-head of our American life."[42]

1927   It is probably during the winter of 1926–27 that Faulkner writes twenty-five pages (17,000 words) of a story entitled "Father Abraham," which he abandons but which constitutes the real point of departure of the chronicle of the Snopes fam-ily.[43] At the same time, he begins on the history of the Sartoris family—the other pole of his novelistic universe. Phil Stone describes the two projects in these terms: "Both are southern in setting. One is something of a saga of an extensive family connection of typical 'poor white trash' and is said by those who have seen that part of the manuscript completed to be the funniest book anybody ever wrote. The other is a tale of the aristocratic, chivalrous and ill-fated Sartoris family, one of whom was even too reckless for the daring Confederate cavalry leader, Jeb Stuart."[44]

11 January   In a letter to Horace Liveright, Faulkner asks for the inclusion of the dedication "To Helen" in *Mosquitoes* (*SLWF*, p. 34).

5 February   Faulkner autographs for Victoria Franklin[45] one of the manuscripts of "The Wishing Tree," a fairy tale not published until after his death.[46]

30 April   *Mosquitoes* is published by Boni and Liveright, on the day the levee of the Mississippi River is blown up in order to save New Orleans from the disastrous flood later described by Faulkner in *The Wild Palms* (1939).

---

[42] William Faulkner, "Foreword," *Sherwood Anderson and Other Famous Creoles: A Gallery of Contemporary New Orleans*, drawn by William M. Spratling and arranged by William C. Faulkner (New Orleans: The Pelican Bookshop, 1926).

[43] For Faulkner's first description of the whole trilogy, see *15 December 1938*. The manuscript of *Father Abraham*, for many years to be read only in the Arents Collection of the New York Public Library, was published in a limited edition of 210 copies edited by James B. Meriwether (New York: Red Ozier Press, 1983), and in a trade facsimile issue (New York: Random House, 1984).

[44] Quoted by James B. Meriwether in "Sartoris and Snopes: An Early Notice," *The Library Chronicle of the University of Texas*, 7 (Summer 1962), 36–39.

[45] See *8 February 1919*.

[46] See *8 April 1967*.

4 May   Helen Baird marries Guy Lyman.

16 July   The *Chicago Tribune* publishes Faulkner's reply to the question: What book would you like to have written? The novelist's choice is *Moby Dick*.[47]

29 September   Date (four days after his thirtieth birthday) on the last page of the typescript of *Flags in the Dust*, which was the original title of the novel to be published in a much-edited and abbreviated form under the title *Sartoris* (1929).[48]

16 October   Faulkner writes to Liveright to announce the novel, which he thinks will be "the damdest best book you'll look at this year, and any other publisher" (*SLWF*, p. 38).

25 November   Letter of rejection by Liveright (*FAB*, p. 560).

30 November   Faulkner writes back, asking that his typescript be returned to him. He adds that he is "working spasmodically on a book which will take three or four years to do ["Father Abraham"?]; also I have started another which I shall finish by spring, I believe" (*SLWF*, p. 39). The latter could be the collection of short stories about which he had written on 18 February.

10 December   Liveright sends back the typescript of *Flags in the Dust*; however, Faulkner is expected to submit his next work to the firm.[49]

1928   Of all the years of Faulkner's life, this is perhaps the *annus mirabilis,* as very little is known of what he did between the beginning of the autumn of 1927, when he finished *Flags in the Dust* and began to try to publish it, and the spring of 1928, when he began *The Sound and the Fury*. It is likely that he did not leave Oxford, at least not for long, and that he spent most of his time writing. "He wrote all the time,"[50] is Phil Stone's

---

[47] The text of this letter can be found in *ESPL*, pp. 197–98.

[48] See *22 August 1973* for publication of the original novel.

[49] There is a sad irony in the fact that he also wrote: "I dont think that even the bird who named 'Soldiers' Pay' can improve on my title," when for the second (though not the last, see *June 1938*) time he would have to give up the title he liked (*SLWF*, p. 38).

[50] Quoted by H. Edward Richardson, *William Faulkner: The Journey to Self-Discovery* (Columbia: University of Missouri Press, 1969), p. 167.

comment, and a very plausible one when one realizes that between novels Faulkner would write many short stories for the commercial market.[51] All that we need to know lies probably in the prefaces which he wrote later to *Sanctuary*[52] and to *The Sound and the Fury*.[53]

27 February At Faulkner's repeated request, Liveright authorizes him to publish *Flags in the Dust* elsewhere. Beginning with this, Faulkner entrusts the sale of his works to his friend Ben Wasson (see *1916*)—which does not keep him, when the need for money is pressing, from mailing stories directly to various magazines.

Spring Faulkner begins *The Sound and the Fury*. The first part is dated "7 April 1928," and the first page of the manuscript bears, as its only title, the word "Twilight," underlined twice.[54]

20 September After probably a dozen attempts to place his manuscript, Faulkner signs a contract with Harcourt, Brace for the publication of *Flags in the Dust* (eventually *Sartoris*), with the proviso that it be reduced to 110,000 words.

October At Ben Wasson's in New York (146 MacDougal Street), Faulkner types the manuscript of *The Sound and the Fury*, revising it in the process according to his habit. It is more than probable that he also helps his friend and agent Wasson edit *Flags in the Dust* in order to make *Sartoris* out of it. He writes to Mrs. McLean, his great-aunt in Memphis, that he has "the damndest book I ever read, I don't believe anyone will publish it for ten years. Harcourt swear they will, but I don't believe it" (*SLWF*, p. 41). Finally, he tries, in vain, to sell

---

[51] See *23 January 1930*.

[52] See the Modern Library edition of the novel (1932).

[53] There were actually two versions of the preface, both written in 1933 for a planned but never produced new edition of the novel. One version, the short one, was published in *The Southern Review* (Fall 1972), 705–10. The longer version was published in *The Mississippi Quarterly*, 26 (Summer 1973), 410–15, and reprinted in *AFM*, pp. 156–61. Both were edited and introduced by James B. Meriwether.

[54] Originally, according to what Faulkner said to his French translator in 1937 (see *20–26 June*), he only intended it as a short story (see *TTWF*, p. 41). However, one can observe that the whole novel, and particularly Quentin's section, is literally drawn toward twilight.

several of his short stories (one of which is called "As I Lay Dying"[55]) to Alfred Dashiell of *Scribner's Magazine.*

12 December   Faulkner is back in Oxford.

27 December   Out of sheer interest in the people, Faulkner follows his uncle, J. W. T. Falkner, Jr., as he campaigns for the post of district attorney (*FAB,* pp. 599–603).

1929   **31 January**   Publication of *Sartoris* by Harcourt, Brace, from whom Faulkner had received an advance of $300 (*FAB,* p. 581). The novel is printed in an edition of 1,998 copies and dedicated to Sherwood Anderson. By this time, Faulkner has begun work on the first version of *Sanctuary.*

18 February   Writing from Oxford to thank him for sending *Sartoris,* Faulkner assures Alfred Harcourt that he does not expect him to take *The Sound and the Fury* and tells him that he has begun another novel *(Sanctuary).* After *The Sound and the Fury* is turned down by Harcourt, Brace (and also probably by Boni & Liveright, since Faulkner was supposed to submit to them the novel he would write after *Flags in the Dust*), Faulkner signs a contract with the new publishing house of Jonathan Cape and Harrison Smith, with an advance of $200 (*FAB,* p. 603).

29 April   Divorce of Estelle Oldham and Cornell Franklin.

6 May   A preliminary contract is signed with Cape and Smith for "a novel." This novel is *Sanctuary,* although the publisher could not have known its identity at the time, since it was not finished.

25 May   The typescript of *Sanctuary* is completed and is immediately turned down by the publisher.[56]

20 June   William Faulkner marries Mrs. Estelle Oldham Franklin in the old Presbyterian church of College Hill, near Oxford. They honeymoon in Pascagoula at the home of Faulkner's friend, Frank H. Lewis, where he corrects the proofs of *The Sound and the Fury* and writes a memorable letter to Ben

---

[55] As in the case of "Afternoon of a Cow" (see *20–26 June 1937*), this story was first published in a French translation by Jacques Pothier, *Sud* 48/49 (1983), 9–28.

[56] For the author's own version of the incident, see his introduction to the 1932 Modern Library edition of the novel.

Wasson (*SLWF,* pp. 44–45). Later, Mrs. Faulkner would re-call that in Pascagoula she tried to read Joyce's *Ulysses* and that, when she complained that it was too difficult, her husband simply said: "Read it again."[57]

Upon their return to Oxford, the Faulkners live at Miss Elma Meek's, on University Avenue, where Faulkner, then working nights at the power plant, writes *As I Lay Dying* "in six weeks, without changing a word"[58]—which is not literally true.

7 October Publication of *The Sound and the Fury,* in an edition of 1,789 copies, by Jonathan Cape and Harrison Smith who, in order to help the book, also publish a limited edition of an essay on the novel by the novelist Evelyn Scott.[59] It is a critical success.

25 October–11 December Dates on the manuscript of *As I Lay Dying* (the first date being the day after the stock exchange crash on Wall Street).

1930 *12 January* The typescript of *As I Lay Dying* is completed.

23 January From this date until some time in January 1932, Faulkner notes on a sheet of cardboard a list of the short stories he tries to sell to national magazines, as well as the dates he submits them. He circles the title of the stories which are accepted and crosses out the titles that are turned down. There is no doubt that, now married and soon to be a house owner, he needs money and that *The Saturday Evening Post* (to whose editor he sent no fewer than thirty-two stories during this two-year period, and which published four of them) paid him more for one story than the total he earned on his first four novels. This precious document bears forty-four titles (with two stories having each two possible titles). Of the forty-two stories submitted, twenty were published or accepted in 1930, 1931, or

---

[57] Mrs. Faulkner to Michel Gresset during a conversation in October 1967 in Charlottesville, Virginia.

[58] See "Introduction" to *Sanctuary* (New York: Modern Library, 1932), p. vii.

[59] *William Faulkner's "The Sound and the Fury"* (New York: Jonathan Cape and Harrison Smith, 1929); reprinted in *TCH,* pp. 76–81).

1932, and ten appeared later. The fact that thirty stories were published out of forty-two submitted is a remarkable achievement.[60]

12 April   Faulkner buys Rowanoak (see *1844*). The acquisition puts him in debt,[61] but it seems to be the expression of a deep wish to set down roots and a kind of deliberate internal exile. The greater part of the books in the library of Rowanoak are dated in his own hand during the years 1930, 1931, and 1932 (*FAB*, p. 668).[62]

30 April   "A Rose for Emily" is published by *Forum*. The first story of his to appear in a national magazine, it is also his most famous (twenty-five reprints in 1970), and the first to appear in French, translated by Maurice Edgar Coindreau in *Commerce* (Winter 1932).

1 May   *Scribner's* buys "Dry September" for $200.

16 May   Date on the first four galleys of the first version of *Sanctuary*, the printing of which is probably interrupted by that of *As I Lay Dying*.

June   Faulkner moves into Rowanoak. *Soldiers' Pay* is published in England with a highly laudatory preface by Richard Hughes.

6 October   *As I Lay Dying* is published in an edition of 2,522 copies by Cape and Smith in New York. The book is dedicated to "Hal [Harrison] Smith."

3 November   Date on sheets five to seventeen of the proofs of the first version of *Sanctuary*.

December   Faulkner, dissatisfied with the first version, sends to Cape and Smith the result of his radical revision of *Sanctuary*.[63]

---

[60] See "Faulkner's Short Story Sending Schedule" in *LCWF*, pp. 167–80.

[61] Until 10 April 1938, according to James W. Webb, "Rowan Oak, Faulkner's Golden Bough," *The University of Mississippi Studies in English*, 6 (1965), 39–47.

[62] See note 25.

[63] The text of the original version was published as *Sanctuary: The Original Text*, ed. Noel Polk (New York: Random House, 1981). For a comparison of the two versions of *Sanctuary*, see Linton R. Massey, "Notes on the Unrevised Galleys of Faulkner's *Sanctuary*," *Studies in Bibliography*, 8 (1956), 195–208; Michael Millgate, " 'A Fair Job': A Study of Faulkner's *Sanctuary*," *Review of English Literature*, 4 (October 1963), 47–62, and his chapter on *Sanctuary* in *The Achievement of William*

12 December   In his speech accepting the Nobel Prize for literature, Sinclair Lewis cites William Faulkner, who has "freed the South from hoop-skirts" (*FAB,* p. 679).

Four stories were published in 1930:
   1. "A Rose for Emily," *Forum,* 83 (April) pp. 233–38; slightly revised for publication in *These 13;*[64] this version reprinted in *CSWF.*[65]
   2. "Honor," *American Mercury,* 20 (July) pp. 268–74; reprinted in *DrM,*[66] and in *CSWF.*
   3. "Thrift," *The Saturday Evening Post,* 203 (6 September) pp. 16ff.; reprinted in *USWF.*
   4. "Red Leaves," *The Saturday Evening Post,* 203 (25 October) pp. 6ff.; revised for *T13;* this version reprinted in *CSWF.*

1931   *1 January:*   On the back of page 7 of the typescript of the short story "The Brooch,"[67] Faulkner writes the amounts he earned in 1930: $200 from *Scribner's* for "Dry September," which was published on 31 January 1931, and twice $750 from *The Saturday Evening Post* for "Thrift" and "Red Leaves." The message was quite clear: he would make more from stories than from novels, and more from *The Saturday Evening Post* than from any other magazine.

11 January   Premature birth of a first child, a daughter named Alabama, who would die on the 16th (or the 20th?).[68] After his visit to the writer in 1937, Maurice Edgar Coindreau noted in his preface to his translation of *The Sound and the Fury*: "Profound emotional shocks are a powerful factor in the inspiration of William Faulkner. It was after the death of one of his children that he wrote *Light in August . . .*"(*TTWF,* p. 49 n.).

9 February   Publication of (the second, revised version of)

Faulkner (New York: Random House, 1965); and Gerald Langford, *Faulkner's Revision of "Sanctuary": A Collation of the Unrevised Galleys and the Published Book* (Austin: University of Texas Press, 1972).
   [64] See *T13.*
   [65] See *CSWF.*
   [66] See *Dr M.*
   [67] This story was published in *Scribner's,* January 1936, pp. 7–12.
   [68] Both dates figure in *FAB:* the first in the genealogy, the second on p. 682. *SLWF* repeats the first, both in the genealogy and in the chronology (p. 466), whereas Minter gives the second in the genealogy of *HLAW.*

Sanctuary by Cape and Smith, in a first printing of 2,219 copies. The book would be Faulkner's best-selling work until *The Wild Palms* (see *March 1939*).

23 March From Princeton, where he has been teaching French literature since 1923, and where he has already translated "Dry September" and "A Rose for Emily," Maurice Edgar Coindreau writes to Faulkner to express his desire to translate *Sanctuary* into French.[69]

1 April: The sales of *Sanctuary* reach 6,457 copies.

14 May Contract signed with Cape and Smith for a collection of stories then entitled *A Rose for Emily and Other Stories*.

June Coindreau's influential introductory article, "William Faulkner," published in *Nouvelle Revue française,* 36, pp. 926–30.[70]

10 July Publication in the Memphis *Press-Scimitar* of the second known interview with Faulkner.[71]

17 August Light in August begun (under the title *Dark House*).[72]

21 September Publication of *These 13* (see *14 May*) by Cape and Smith, in an edition of 1,928 copies. The book is dedicated to "Estelle and Alabama."

23–24 October Faulkner attends a meeting of southern writers in Charlottesville, Virginia. Sherwood Anderson, who also attends, writes to a correspondent on the 24th: "Bill Faulkner had arrived and got drunk. From time to time he appeared, got drunk again immediately, and disappeared. He kept asking everyone for drinks. If they didn't give him any, he drank his own."[73]

---

[69] However, Gallimard had already contracted with René-Noël Raimbault for this translation, which was published in November 1932, whereas Maurice Edgar Coindreau's version of *As I Lay Dying,* which was ready in 1932, had to wait until April 1934 to be published.

[70] Translation by George M. Reeves in *TTWF,* pp. 25–30.

[71] This interview, obtained by Marshall Smith, was published a second time, in a slightly different version, in *The Bookman* (December 1931). Both versions are given in *LITG*.

[72] For a second tentative use of the same title, see *January or February 1934*.

[73] *The Letters of Sherwood Anderson,* p. 252.

Thus one is confronted with the question of Faulkner's alcoholism. It is true that Faulkner drank, sometimes heavily, and that he kept up the habit until his death. However, a few points should be made here. First, he certainly did not lack examples in his own family. As his brother Murry wrote, "Our father, in common with a goodly portion of the rest of the male members of our clan, was singularly free from an aversion to the bottle, and this led him, from time to time, to become a guest at the Cure"[74] (*TFOM,* p. 45). Second, if he, like many other Americans who have daily cocktails, drank regularly, what characterizes his drinking was certainly its excesses, which came on suddenly and in bouts. These left him all but unconscious, at which point he often had to be taken for "the Cure" or to a hospital.[75] Third, it is difficult, if not even impossible, to believe that there was not, at least generally, a rather strict line of separation between his drinking and writing. As his brother John noted: "But no man could turn out the amount of work Bill did and drink as much as people claim he did" (*MBB,* pp. 149–50). If proof were needed, an examination of the manuscripts would furnish it. As Faulkner got older, however, it is clear that it did occasionally interfere with his work. This is the impression that Coindreau got after his visit to the writer in California, in 1937 (*FAB,* pp. 717–21).

Be that as it may, the most striking feature of Faulkner's alcoholism is that it was quite different from what one knows about other writers of the "lost generation"; for Hemingway, in particular, drinking was above all a social, collective manifestation of "mal du siècle," whereas for Faulkner it seems to have resulted from a profound feeling of solitude that often became unbearable. What heartrending, what incurable despair did the drinking hide? Perhaps nothing can ever say it better than the books themselves.

---

[74] An establishment known as the "Keeley Cure," fifteen miles from Memphis.

[75] "Mr. Acarius," a story published after Faulkner's death (see *9 October 1965*), reveals the author's familiarity with this type of residence (*USWF,* pp. 435–48). On Faulkner's alcoholism, see *FAB,* pp. 717–21.

26 October   Faulkner arrives in New York from Charlottesville in company with Harrison Smith. At once, several publishers (Alfred Knopf, Harold Guinzburg, Bennett Cerf, and Donald Klopfer, the latter two having just founded Random House) are anxious to court the author of *Sanctuary*. At Smith's instigation, Faulkner flees, first to Florida, then to North Carolina.

4 November   Faulkner is back in New York, where he spends several weeks. He finds out to his own surprise that he is "now the most important figure in American letters." He meets other writers, among them Nathanael West, Dashiell Hammett, and Lillian Hellman. And, according to a letter to his wife Estelle, he is going to be invited to work in Hollywood for "$500.00 or 750.00 a week" (*SLWF*, pp. 52–53).

9 November   He inscribes a copy of *As I Lay Dying*, "With gratitude, to Dr. Coindreau, the translator."

13 November   In another enthusiastic letter to his wife, he writes from New York: "Even Sinclair Lewis and Dreiser make engagements to see me, and Mencken. . . ." He says that he has almost finished a "play from *Sanctuary*" (which has been lost), and "a movie for Tallulah Bankhead. How's that for high?" (*SLWF*, p. 53). Two interviews are published, one by the *New York Herald Tribune* (14 November), and one by *The New Yorker* (28 November). In both he repeats what he has already said in Virginia, that the two books he likes best are *Moby Dick* and *The Nigger of the Narcissus* (*LITG*, p. 21).

30 November   In Memphis, en route to New York where she is to join her husband, Mrs. Faulkner announces that her husband is going to Hollywood.

10 December   After the publication of the story *Idyll in the Desert* by Random House in a limited edition of 400 copies, Mr. and Mrs. Faulkner leave New York for Baltimore where H. L. Mencken has invited them before going back home.

18 December   Sam Marx, of Metro-Goldwyn-Mayer, approaches Faulkner, who has just returned home after eight weeks.

A record number of sixteen stories were published in 1931:

1. "Dry September," *Scribner's,* 89 (January) pp. 49–56; revised for insertion in *T13*; this version reprinted in *CSWF*.

2. "That Evening Sun Go Down," *American Mercury,* 22 (March) pp. 257–67; revised for *T13,* under the title "That Evening Sun"; this version reprinted in *CSWF*.

3. "Ad Astra," *American Caravan,* 4 (27 March) pp. 164–81; revised for *T13*; this version reprinted in *CSWF*.

4. "Hair," *American Mercury,* 23 (May) pp. 53–61; revised for *T13;* this version reprinted in *CSWF*.

5. "Spotted Horses," *Scribner's,* 89 (June) pp. 585–97; incorporated in *The Hamlet* (1940) after extensive revision.

6. "The Hound," *Harper's,* 163 (August) pp. 263–74; reprinted in *DrM*; incorporated in *The Hamlet* (1940) after revision.

7. "Fox Hunt," *Harper's,* 163 (September) pp. 392–402; reprinted in *DrM,* then in *CSWF*.

8. "All the Dead Pilots," *T13* (21 September); reprinted in *CSWF*.

9. "Carcassonne," *T13* (21 September); reprinted in *CSWF*.

10. "Crevasse," *T13* (21 September); reprinted in *CSWF*.

11. "Divorce in Naples," *T13* (21 September); reprinted in *CSWF*.

12. "A Justice," *T13* (21 September); reprinted in *CSWF*.

13. "Mistral," *T13* (21 September); reprinted in *CSWF*.

14. "Victory," *T13* (21 September); reprinted in *CSWF*.

15. "Doctor Martino," *Harper's,* 163 (November) pp. 733–43; reprinted in *DrM* and in *CSWF*.

16. *Idyll in the Desert* (10 December), New York: Random House.

1932 *1 February* An issue of a "little magazine," *Contempo,* published in Chapel Hill, North Carolina (where Faulkner had visited in the fall of the preceding year, see *26 October 1931*), is devoted almost entirely to his work, with nine poems and a story ("Once Aboard A Lugger"[76]), a review of *These 13* and *Idyll in the Desert,* and a short presentation in which, after a comparison with Sinclair Lewis, Sherwood Anderson, Theodore Dreiser, John Dos Passos, Evelyn Scott (see *7 October 1929*), Ernest Hemingway, and Willa Cather, he is called "the most creative of contemporary American writers."

---

[76] See the list of stories published in 1932.

14 February   Henry Nash Smith publishes an interview with Faulkner in the Dallas *Morning News.* In spite of Faulkner's declaration that he has never read *Ulysses,* Smith notes that he owns an edition dated 1924.[77]

19 February   Faulkner completes the manuscript of *Light in August.*

March   Publication of the Modern Library edition of *Sanctuary,* with a well-known, though generally misunderstood,[78] introduction by the author. Meanwhile, his royalties from the sale of the novel ($4,000) are frozen because of the liquidation of the firm of Cape and Smith. This may explain why, when Faulkner sends the typescript of *Light in August* to his agent Ben Wasson, he asks him to try and serialize it, adding: "I will not want to take less than $5,000 for it, and not a word to be changed" (*SLWF,* p. 61).

14 April   First and most important letter to Maurice Edgar Coindreau from Oxford, thanking the French translator for sending his versions of "Dry September" and of "A Rose for Emily," as well as for his article of June 1931 in the *Nouvelle Revue française,* which "a friend in Paris" had sent him. "I see now," Faulkner writes, "that I have a quite decided strain of puritanism (in its proper sense, of course; not our American one) regarding sex. I was not aware of it."[79]

April   Faulkner signs a six-week contract with Metro-Goldwyn-Mayer, to become effective 7 May.[80]

7 May–16 June   First "stint" as a scriptwriter in Hollywood,

---

[77] This is borne out by the fact that he owned a copy of the fourth printing (January 1924) of the Paris, Shakespeare and Company edition, autographed "William Faulkner / Rowan Oak, 1924." See *WFLAC,* p. 77, *LIG,* p. 30, and also *20 June 1929* in this chronology.

[78] The second sentence, "To me it is a cheap idea, because it was deliberately conceived to make money," was interpreted for many years as referring to the aesthetic outcome of the rewriting of the original version, when in fact it was a self-critical, ethical judgment upon the genesis of the first version and upon the author's reasons for writing it.

[79] A facsimile of this letter was published in *The Princeton University Library Chronicle,* 18 (Spring 1957). The text was reprinted in *SLWF,* pp. 63–64.

[80] Thirteen years later, in 1945, when he had finally succeeded in freeing himself from the last and most arduous of his contracts with Hollywood, Faulkner had spent a total of almost four years at "the salt mines." See *FIH.*

at $500 a week. On 16 June, Paramount takes an option on *Sanctuary*.

27 June   Publication of *Miss Zilphia Gant* by the Texas Book Club in an edition limited to 300 copies, with a preface by Henry Nash Smith.

July   In Hollywood, where he is trying to make more money, Faulkner meets Howard Hawks. The two men, who have in common a passion for flying and hunting, get along well.[81] It was Hawks's brother William who recommended the film adaptation of the story "Turn About" (published on 5 March by *The Saturday Evening Post*).[82] Faulkner's contract with MGM is renewed, though only at $250 a week—an amount which Faulkner had refused when Sam Marx offered it for a whole year.

21 July   Composition of *Light in August* is completed. When reading proof, Faulkner refuses to make a good many of the suggested corrections.

7 August   Faulkner's stay in Hollywood is interrupted by the death of his father.

25 September   Faulkner writes to Ben Wasson from Oxford to say that he has had to leave California without being able to complete his adaptation of "Turn About," and he expresses the hope that Paramount will film *Sanctuary* (the contract was signed on 17 October). Faulkner needed money; his father had left his mother with hardly more than a year's living. "Then it's me," he wrote to Ben Wasson (*SLWF*, p. 65).

3 October   Faulkner is back in California with his mother and his younger brother Dean.

6 October   Publication of *Light in August* by the new publishing house founded by Harrison Smith and Robert Haas. With

---

[81] Hawks said: "Bill and I were good friends. We hunted and fished together. I bought the first story he had sold. . . . We worked together on a half dozen films. I could call him any time to ask him for a scene and he always gave it to me" (Joseph McBride, ed., *Focus on Howard Hawks*. Englewood Cliffs, N.J.: Prentice-Hall, 1972, pp. 21–22). And Faulkner said later: "Whenever I needed the money, Mr. Hawks was always very good to me, and if he needs me now, I'm going." See *FIH*, p. 264.

[82] See chapter 4 of *FAF*.

480 pages, the book is the longest Faulkner has written so far; however, he did not get as much satisfaction from it as he had from *The Sound and the Fury*.[83]

22 October   Having earned $6,000 in Hollywood, Faulkner returns to Mississippi.

28 November–13 May 1933   Thanks to Howard Hawks's mediation with MGM, Faulkner is paid $600 a week, even though he remains in Oxford.

8 December   Bennett Cerf offers $500 for an introduction to a limited edition of *The Sound and the Fury* to be printed by the Grabhorn Press.

23 December   Harrison Smith begs Faulkner in vain for an introduction to *A Green Bough*, Faulkner's second and last volume of poetry.

Eight stories were published in 1932:

1. "Death-Drag," *Scribner's*, 91 (January) pp. 34–42; slightly revised for collection, under the title "Death Drag," in *DrM*; this version reprinted in *CSWF*.

2. "Centaur in Brass," *American Mercury*, 25 (February) pp. 200–10; reprinted in *CSWF*; incorporated in *The Town* (1957).

3. "Once Aboard the Lugger," *Contempo*, I (1 February) pp. 1ff.; reprinted, along with another, probably later, version, in *USWF*.

4. "Lizards in Jamshyd's Courtyard," *The Saturday Evening Post*, 204 (27 February) pp. 12ff.; incorporated in *The Hamlet* (1940).

5. "Turn About," *The Saturday Evening Post*, 204 (5 March) pp. 6ff.; revised for collection in *DrM*; this version, entitled "Turnabout," reprinted in *CSWF*.

6. "Smoke," *Harper's*, 164 (April), pp. 562–78; slightly revised for insertion in *DrM*; this version reprinted in *Knight's Gambit* (1949).

7. *Miss Zilphia Gant*, Dallas: Book Club of Texas (27 June), limited edition of 300 copies; reprinted in *USWF*.

8. "A Mountain Victory," *The Saturday Evening Post*, 205 (3 December) pp. 6ff.; revised, under the title "Mountain Victory," for collection in *DrM*; this version reprinted in *CSWF*.

1933 *January*   Faulkner declines Bennett Cerf's offer (now raised to $750) to write an introduction for the new, limited

---

[83] See the shorter of the two versions of his introduction to *The Sound and the Fury* in *The Southern Review*, 8 (Autumn 1972), 708–10.

edition of *The Sound and the Fury*; at the moment, he does not have a pressing need for money. In fact, he has just published "There Was a Queen" in *Scribner's,* and on 12 February he writes to Ben Wasson: "I have enough money now to finish my house" (*SLWF,* p. 70).

27 February   Date on the final proofs of *A Green Bough.*

25 March   The Memphis *Commercial Appeal* announces that "the writer is learning to fly." Ever since 2 February, Faulkner has been coming from Oxford every week to take flying lessons with Captain Vernon Omlie.

12 April   Premiere in Memphis, with Faulkner attending, of *Today We Live,* the film made from "Turn About" by Howard Hawks, with Joan Crawford, Gary Cooper, Franchot Tone. See *FAF,* chapter 4.

20 April   Faulkner solos, "most probably, for the first time," Blotner comments (*FAB,* p. 797). Publication of *A Green Bough* by Smith and Haas in New York, consisting of forty-four loosely connected poems, most of them dating from the 1920s.

28 April   Opening of *Today We Live,* the only production by MGM in which Faulkner's name appears in the credits.

5 May   Faulkner is in New Orleans, working on a film entitled *Louisiana Lou* (to be released later as *Lazy River*).

12 May   Opening of the film *The Story of Temple Drake,* made from *Sanctuary* by Stephen Roberts for Paramount. Faulkner did not participate in writing the adaptation. This is the rule he observed for the films, generally mediocre, which were made from his novels; he broke it only with the script of *Intruder in the Dust* (see *Spring 1949*).

13 May   Expiration of the contract signed with MGM in April 1932. At home, Faulkner, who has now more money than ever before in his bank account, buys a Waco-210 monoplane.

24 June   Jill Faulkner, only daughter of the author, is born.

27 June   Faulkner announces his daughter's birth to Ben Wasson in the following terms: "Well, bud, we've got us a baby gal named Jill. Born Saturday and both well." He adds: "About Bennett [Cerf] and 'Sound & F.' All right. Let me know about it, if he will use the colored ink. I like that. I will need time to lay it out again. How many different colors shall I be limited to? Just what does he want in the introduction? I'm ready to start right away. $750.00 is right, is it?"[84] He also asks: "What about the Cape & Smith business? Is all that lost?"[85] And he concludes: "Working spasmodically at a novel" (*SLWF*, p. 71).

11 August   According to the Memphis *Press-Scimitar*, "the author of *Sanctuary* finds peace in the sky." Faulkner is also reported as saying: "I made about $35,000 out of my movie work, but it's a rotten way to make a living."

29 August   Bennett Cerf receives the copy of *The Sound and the Fury* prepared by Faulkner for the projected Grabhorn edition of this novel in three colors, while the text of the introduction referred to in his letter of 27 June goes to Ben Wasson. However, the project falls through, and the copy of the novel marked by the author is, unfortunately, lost.

October   To Harrison Smith, who has recently inquired about a novel, Faulkner replies: "I have been at the Snopes book, but I have another bee now, and a good title, I think: REQUIEM FOR A NUN. It will be about a nigger woman. It will be a little on the esoteric side, like AS I LAY DYING" (*SLWF*, p. 75). These prospects, as well as a new collection of stories, are the subject of a conversation between Smith and Faulkner on the occasion of Jill's baptism, later the same month. Obviously, when Faulkner wanted money and as he never made much with his novels, he had (as he wrote in the same letter) only two options: "write [and sell] a short story every so often or go back to Hollywood."

3 November   Accompanied by his brother Dean and by Vernon Omlie, Faulkner flies to New York.

14 December   Faulkner receives his pilot's wings (No. 29788).

17 December   The date written at the beginning of the manuscript of a novel entitled "Requiem for a Nun." Faulk-

---

[84] *SLWF*, p. 71. See *8 December 1932* and *January 1933*.

[85] "The royalties owed to Faulkner were lost when Cape & Smith went into receivership." See *SLWF*, p. 71.

ner's literary agent is now Morton Goldman, a former associate of Ben Wasson's.

In 1933, three stories were published:

1. "There Was a Queen," *Scribner's,* 93 (January) pp. 10–16; reprinted in *DrM* and in *CSWF.*

2. "Artist at Home," *Story,* 3 (August) pp. 27–41; reprinted in *CSWF.*

3. "Beyond," *Harper's,* 167 (September) pp. 394–403; reprinted in *DrM* and in *CSWF.*

1934 *January or February* Faulkner writes to Harrison Smith: "I believe that I have a head start on the novel. I have put both the Snopes and the Nun one aside. The one I am writing now will be called DARK HOUSE or something of that nature. It is the more or less violent breakup of a household or family from 1860 to about 1910. It is not as heavy as it sounds. The story is an anecdote which occurred during and right after the civil war; the climax is another anecdote which happened about 1910 and which explains the story. Roughly, the theme is a man who outraged the land, and the land then turned and destroyed the man's family. Quentin Compson, of the Sound & Fury, tells it, or ties it together; he is the protagonist so that it is not complete apocrypha. I use him because it is just before he is to commit suicide because of his sister, and I use his bitterness which he has projected on the South in the form of hatred of it and its people to get more out of the story itself than a historical novel would be. To keep the hoop skirts and plug hats out, you might say. I believe I can promise it for fall" (*SLWF,* pp. 78–79). Perhaps the most interesting portion of this remarkable sketch of *Absalom, Absalom!* is the sentence about the use of "Quentin Compson, of the Sound & Fury."

14 February: Ash Wednesday Captain Merle Nelson is killed during an air show in New Orleans at the inauguration of the "Colonel A. L. Shushan" Airport. Faulkner and Vernon Omlie arrive from Memphis the following day.

1 April The first issue of the *Oxford Magazine* publishes the first part of a long study by Phil Stone entitled "William Faulkner, the Man and His Work," in which the author assumes a rather ambiguous stance of both protection and bitterness with regard to his former protégé.[86]

16 April   Publication of a second collection of stories, *Doctor Martino and Other Stories,* by Smith and Haas. The volume contains only two previously unpublished stories, "The Leg" and "Black Music."

Spring   Faulkner begins a series of stories about the Civil War to be sold to *The Saturday Evening Post* and later to be collected under the title *The Unvanquished.*

1 June   The second part of Phil Stone's study is published.

1–24 July   Faulkner is in Hollywood, where he has accepted an offer from Universal Studios at $1,000 a week. He works with Howard Hawks on an adaptation of Blaise Cendrars' *L'Or (Sutter's Gold),* "a project first tackled by Eisenstein. That film never got past the treatment stage—although it may well have influenced Faulkner's plans for *Absalom, Absalom!"* (*FAF,* p. 88).

"Thursday" (August)   In a letter to Harrison Smith, Faulkner writes: "I believe that the book is not quite ripe yet; that I have not gone my nine months, you might say. I do have to put it aside and make a nickel every so often, but I think there must be more than that. I have a mass of stuff, but only one chapter that suits me; I am considering putting it aside and going back to REQUIEM FOR A NUN, which will be a short one, like AS I LAY DYING, while the present one will probably be longer than LIGHT IN AUGUST. I have a title for it which I like, by the way: ABSALOM, ABSALOM; the story is of a man who wanted a son through pride, and got too many of them and they destroyed him . . . (*SLWF,* pp. 83–84).

September   Faulkner completes and sends directly to *The Saturday Evening Post* the story entitled "The Unvanquished" (later to be retitled "Riposte in Tertio"). He begins work on "Vendée."

29 September–3 November   "Ambuscade," "Retreat," and

---

[86] Reprinted by James B. Meriwether in "Early Notices of Faulkner by Phil Stone and Louis Cochran," *The Mississippi Quarterly,* 17 (Summer 1964), 136–64.

"Raid" (the first three chapters of the future book) appear successively in *The Saturday Evening Post*.

4 October   "Drusilla" is sent to *The Saturday Evening Post* and "Vendée" is revised to suit the wishes of the editors.

1 November   The third and last part of the Stone study is published in the *Oxford Magazine*, which ceases publication.

11 November–15 December   Faulkner sends to Harrison Smith successively the seven chapters of *Pylon*, a work apparently inspired by the events of the previous 14 February.[87]

During 1934, eleven stories were published for the first time:

1. "Elly," *Story*, 4 (February) pp. 3–15; reprinted in *DrM* and in *CSWF*.

2. "Pennsylvania Station," *American Mercury*, 31 (February) pp. 166–74; reprinted in *CSWF*.

3. "Wash," *Harper's*, 168 (February) pp. 258–66; reprinted in *DrM* and in *CSWF;* incorporated in *Absalom, Absalom!* (1936).

4. "A Bear Hunt," *The Saturday Evening Post*, 206 (10 February) pp. 8ff.; reprinted in *CSWF*; revised for insertion in *Big Woods* (1955).

5. "Black Music," *DrM* (16 April); reprinted in *CSWF*.

6. "Leg," *DrM* (16 April); reprinted in *CSWF* under the title "The Leg."

7. "Mule in the Yard," *Scribner's*, 96 (August) pp. 65–70; reprinted in *CSWF*; incorporated in *The Town* (1957).

8. "Ambuscade," *The Saturday Evening Post*, 207 (29 September) pp. 12ff.; revised for *The Unvanquished* (1938); magazine version reprinted in *USWF*.

9. "Retreat," *The Saturday Evening Post*, 207 (13 October) pp. 16ff.; revised for *The Unvanquished* (1938); magazine version reprinted in *USWF*.

10. "Lo!" *Story*, 5 (November) pp. 5–21; reprinted in *CSWF*.

11. "Raid," *The Saturday Evening Post*, 207 (3 November) p. 18.; revised for *The Unvanquished* (1938); magazine version reprinted in *USWF*.

1935   **9 January**   The eighty-four pages of galley proof of *Pylon* are ready.

Mid-January   Harrison Smith comes to Oxford to read over

---

[87] See Michael Millgate's research on this in *TAWF*, pp. 138–49.

the novel with the author: "There are things in it that need to be changed, but only here and there" (*FAB,* p. 876).

5 February   Faulkner receives from Smith and Haas an advance of $2,000 on *Absalom, Absalom!*

18 February   Faulkner declines several offers: an edition of *The Marionettes*[88] ("NO, absolutely NOT"); a book on the Mississippi River ("I am a novelist, you see: people first, where second"); and an article on lynching ("Tell them [he writes to his agent] I never saw a lynching and so couldn't describe one") (*SLWF,* p. 89).

25 March   Publication of *Pylon* by Smith and Haas.

30 March   Date on the first page of the final manuscript of *Absalom, Absalom!*[89] As he did with *Pylon,* Faulkner sends the first chapter as soon as it is typed.

March[?]   Faulkner sends the story "Lion" to Morton Goldman, who sells it to *Harper's.* This story was the beginning of a creative process that would eventually result in the publication of *Go Down, Moses* (1942) (see *note 115, V, 1).*

29 June   Harrison Smith receives chapter two of *Absalom, Absalom!*

22 July   Smith receives chapter three of *Absalom, Absalom!* In a letter to Morton Goldman, Faulkner, once more "under pressure" for money, offers to sell his manuscripts: "besides the short stories, I have SOUND & FURY, AS I LAY DYING, SANCTUARY, LIGHT IN AUGUST, PYLON. Will there be any market for it?" he asks, before ending his letter with the following confidence: "I am trying to get the novel done as soon as possible, so that when I come East I can make a better contract than I have. Keep this under your hat, of course" (*SLWF* p. 92). Some time before, probably in March, he had already written to his agent a letter in which he said: "But I cannot and will not go on like this. I believe I have got enough fair literature in me yet to deserve reasonable freedom from

---

[88] See note 22.

[89] This manuscript is a composite since it includes paste-ins and newly written pages. After Faulkner had donated it to the cause of Republican Spain (see *24 October 1939*), and after being bought (for $260!) and sold again, it finally wound up, after a detour by way of England, at the University of Texas at Austin.

bourgeoise [sic] material petty impediments and compulsion, without having to quit writing and go to the moving pictures every two years. The trouble about the movies is not so much the time I waste there but the time it takes me to recover and settle down again; I am 37 now and of course not as supple and impervious as I once was" (*SLWF,* p. 90).

19 August   Harrison Smith receives chapter 4 of *Absalom, Absalom!*

23 September   Faulkner leaves for New York with a view to bettering his financial situation. He gets a loan from Smith, which he will repay by going to work for eight weeks in Hollywood.

13 October   Faulkner returns to Oxford.

15 October   Date on page one of the manuscript of chapter 5 of *Absalom, Absalom!*

10 November   Faulkner's younger brother, Dean, who had become a professional pilot with the support of the novelist and had married Louise Hale only a month before, is killed in the crash of the Waco his brother had given him. The novelist would take complete responsibility for the education of his niece, who was born on 22 March 1936 and given her father's first name. Carvel Collins and Joseph Blotner, among others, agree that Faulkner wrote the second half of *Absalom, Absalom!* while overwhelmingly grief-stricken. According to Blotner, he wrote it in the evenings on the dining table in his mother's house in Oxford, where Dean's widow had come to live (*FAB,* p. 917)

December   In California, Howard Hawks, now at Twentieth Century-Fox, offers Faulkner a new contract to go into effect on 16 December at $1,000 a week. Faulkner signs it. This begins his second major "tour of duty" in Hollywood, one not much more interesting than the first, although he is better paid (*FIH,* p. 273). He works "intermittently" on an adaptation of *Les Croix de bois (Wooden Crosses),* a World War I novel by the French novelist Roland Dorgelès, and he works "furiously" on *Absalom, Absalom!* This is also the time of the beginning of his liaison with Meta Carpenter, Howard Hawks's pretty secretary and script girl.

4 December   From Oxford, Faulkner writes to Morton Goldman: "I am working like hell now. The novel is pretty good and I think another month will see it done" (*SLWF,* p. 93).

31 December   In Hollywood, Faulkner and Joel Sayre complete the screenplay of *Wooden Crosses,* renamed *Zero Hour,* then *The Road to Glory,* but little was kept of their collaboration in the film which was released, after many changes, on 2 June 1936.

Five stories were published in 1935:

1. "Skirmish at Sartoris," *Scribner's,* 97 (April) pp. 193–200; revised for *The Unvanquished* (1938); magazine version reprinted in *USWF.*

2. "Golden Land," *American Mercury,* 35 (May) pp. 1–14; reprinted in *CSWF.*

3. "That Will Be Fine," *American Mercury,* 35 (July) pp. 264–76; reprinted in *CSWF.*

4. "Uncle Willy," *American Mercury,* 36 (October) pp. 156–68; reprinted in *CSWF.*

5. "Lion," *Harper's,* 172 (December) pp. 67–77; considerably revised and expanded for inclusion in *Go Down, Moses* (1942) under the title "The Bear."

1936   *31 January*   Back at Rowan Oak, Faulkner completes and dates the manuscript of *Absalom, Absalom!*[90] There follows his first stay at the nursing home in Byhalia, Mississippi (see *6 July 1962*). Random House buys the firm of Harrison Smith and Robert Haas; Smith and Haas thus become the associates of Bennett Cerf and Donald Klopfer.

26 February   At Movietone City, Faulkner is on Twentieth Century-Fox's payroll again, assigned to work on *Banjo on My Knee.*

7 March   In a letter to Stark Young, Thomas Wolfe writes of Faulkner that "what he writes is not like the South, and yet the South is in his books and in the spirit that created them."[91]

22 March   Dean, the daughter of Dean Falkner and Louise Hale, is born.

---

[90] See preceding note.
[91] Elizabeth Nowell, ed., *The Letters of Thomas Wolfe* (New York: Scribners, 1956), p. 495.

Spring   At Stanley Rose's Bookshop in Hollywood, Faulkner meets Nathanael West. The two go hunting together.

Mid-May   Faulkner is back at Rowan Oak in time for Jill's third birthday.

22 June   The following notice, signed by Faulkner, is published in the Memphis *Commercial Appeal:* "I will not be responsible for any debt incurred or bills made, or notes or checks signed by Mrs. William Faulkner or Mrs. Estelle Oldham Faulkner" (*FAB,* p. 938).

15 July   Faulkner leaves for Hollywood again, this time with his wife and daughter.

4 September   From Beverly Hills, Faulkner writes to his agent, Morton Goldman: "As you see, I am in California again up to my neck in moving pictures, where I shall be for about a year"—and he adds: "I am going to undertake to sell this book [*Absalom, Absalom!*] myself to the pictures, first. I am going to ask one hundred thousand dollars for it or nothing, as I do not need to sell it now since I have a job." And in a letter written on the same day to his editor Harrison Smith, he asks for a set of "clean galleys" (*SLWF,* p. 96). Joseph Blotner writes: "One day Nunnally Johnson [the producer] entered his office to find the galleys on his desk with a note in Faulkner's neat and difficult handwriting. It read: 'Nunnally—These are the proofs of my new book. The price is $50,000. It's about miscegenation. Bill.' But 1936 was not Hollywood's year for miscegenation or *Absalom, Absalom!,* and nothing came out of Faulkner's sales campaign" (*FIH,* pp. 277–78).

26 October   Publication of *Absalom, Absalom!* by Random House in an edition of 6,000 copies plus a limited edition of 300. Copy number one was inscribed by Faulkner "for Meta Carpenter, wherever she may be" (*FAB,* p. 947).[92]

25 December   The Faulkners celebrate Christmas in Pacific Palisades.

28 December   Faulkner writes to Bennett Cerf: "I have a series of six stories about a white boy and a negro boy during

---

[92] From this date, with the few exceptions that are noted, all of Faulkner's books were to be published by Random House.

the civil war. . . . What do you think about getting them out as book?" (*SLWF*, pp. 97–98; the book would be *The Unvanquished*).

Five stories were published in 1936:

1. "The Brooch," *Scribner's,* 99 (January) pp. 7–12; reprinted in *CSWF.*

2. "Two Dollar Wife," *College Life,* 18 (January) pp. 8ff.; reprinted in *USWF.*

3. "Fool About A Horse," *Scribner's* 100 (August) pp. 80–86; incorporated in *The Hamlet* (1940); magazine version reprinted in *USWF.*

4. "The Unvanquished," *The Saturday Evening Post,* 209 (14 November) pp. 12ff.; revised and entitled "Riposte in Tertio" for *The Unvanquished*; magazine version reprinted in *USWF.*

5. "Vendée," *The Saturday Evening Post,* 209 (5 December) pp. 16ff.; revised for *The Unvanquished*; magazine version reprinted in *USWF.*

1937 *Winter 1936–1937*   After working on *Gunga Din,* then on *The Last Slaver* (later *Slave Ship*), Faulkner is assigned to *Splinter Fleet,* to *Dance Hall,* and finally to *Drums Along the Mohawk,* all for Twentieth Century-Fox and all without credit. At the end of the winter, he takes his family to a new house in Beverly Hills, where Maurice Edgar Coindreau visits him.

26 February   Faulkner writes to Coindreau that "After reading 'As I Lay Dying' in your translation, I am happy that you are considering undertaking S&F." He even offers "to draw up a chronology and genealogy and explanation, etc. if you need it, or anything else" (*SLWF,* p. 99).

18 March   Faulkner's weekly wages at Twentieth Century-Fox go up from $750 to $1,000.

5 April   Meta Carpenter (née Doherty) marries Wolfgang Rebner and follows him to Germany (*HAC,* p. 87).

May   Faulkner hires a chauffeur to take his wife and daughter back home to Mississippi.

20–26 June   Coindreau spends a week with Faulkner, at 129 Ledoux Boulevard in Beverly Hills, working on the French translation of *The Sound and the Fury.* When he leaves, Faulkner makes him a gift of the typescript of a sketch entitled "Afternoon of a Cow," which he signed with a parodical pseudonym, "Ernest V. Trueblood."[93]

24 July Faulkner writes to Morton Goldman: "Random House is going to collect the Civil War stories we sold the Post into a book. They needed one more story to finish them, which I have just completed, named 'An Odor of Verbena'" (*SLWF*, p. 100).

28 July Faulkner writes to his wife: "Nothing has happened yet. As far as I know, I will be through at studio Aug 15 and will start home sometime during that week . . . It's hot here and I dont feel very good, but I think it's mostly being tired of movies, worn out with them" (*SLWF*, p. 101).

1 September Faulkner is back at Rowan Oak after a partly idle year at Twentieth Century-Fox, which had paid him $21,650 since January.

15 September Faulkner dates the first page of the holograph manuscript of *The Wild Palms*. "Shortly after that, when Meta and Wolfgang Rebner returned to New York from their honeymoon in Europe, Faulkner met them at the dock," Carvel Collins writes (*HAC*, pp. 88–89).

Mid-October In New York, Faulkner meets Saxe Commins, who is to become his editor at Random House. He sees Sherwood Anderson again. He also drinks a lot and in November is severely burned by a steam pipe at his hotel.

17 November Interviewed by the Memphis *Commercial Appeal*, Faulkner says he does not intend to return to Hollywood because "I don't know enough about it. I feel as though I can't do myself justice in that type of work" (*LITG*, p. 34). (He would not return to Hollywood until the summer of 1942.)

21 December Faulkner writes to Robert Haas: "The novel *The Wild Palms* is coming pretty well; I found less trouble than I anticipated in getting back into the habit of writing, though

---

[93] See Coindreau's recollection of his visit to Faulkner in "The Faulkner I Knew," *TTWF*, pp. 91–102. The sketch was published in Coindreau's translation in *Fontaine* (Algiers), June–July 1943, before it appeared in the original version in *Furioso*, 2 (Summer 1947), 5–17.

I find that at forty I dont write quite as fast as I used to. It should be done by May first though" (*SLWF*, p. 102).

Winter 1937–1938   Almost simultaneously, Faulkner acquires "Bailey's Woods," a property adjoining Rowan Oak, and "Greenfield Farm," located seventeen miles from Oxford, the management of which he turns over to his brother John. From then on, he could say with some degree of truth that he was "a farmer who told stories."[94]

Only one story was published in 1937:
   "Monk," *Scribner's*, 101 (May) pp. 16–24; reprinted in *Knight's Gambit* (1949).

1938   *15 February*   Publication of *The Unvanquished,* a volume consisting of seven stories: the first six, published originally from September 1934 to December 1936, were revised for publication in book form (the first five of these six stories had appeared in *The Saturday Evening Post,* the sixth in *Scribner's*); the last, "An Odor of Verbena," appears for the first time. The book is illustrated by Edward Shenton.

16 February   The rights on *The Unvanquished* are ceded to MGM for $25,000, 20 percent of which are to go to Random House.

May   Faulkner is one of 418 notable Americans to respond to a letter seeking reactions to the Spanish Civil War: "I most sincerely wish to go on record as being unalterably opposed to Franco and fascism, to all violations of the legal government and outrages against the people of Republican Spain" (*ESPL,* p. 198).

June   Faulkner sends Random House the typescript of the novel to be entitled *The Wild Palms.* In a letter to Joan Williams dated 8 August 1952, he would write: ". . . I remembered how I wrote THE WILD PALMS in order to try to stave off what I thought was heart-break too" (*SLWF,* p. 338).[95]

September–October   In New York, where he has come to read

---

[94] See both *FITU* and *LITG* for comments on this subject.

[95] See "Biographical Background for Faulkner's *Helen,*" Carvel Collins's introduction to *HAC,* pp. 86–96, for a carefully detailed identification of Charlotte Rittenmeyer with Helen Baird.

the proofs of the novel (which would be published with the title *The Wild Palms* and not *If I Forget thee, Jerusalem*,[96] which was the original title), Faulkner types a story—most probably "Barn Burning."

7 November Faulkner resumes work on "Barn Burning," this time striking out this title at the top of the handwritten page on which he now writes "Book One, Chapter I."[97] This indicates that he originally meant "Barn Burning" to be the opening chapter of his next novel, *The Hamlet.*

19 November Faulkner sends "Barn Burning" to Harold Ober, who becomes his agent from this time on; Ober sells the story to *Harper's* for $400.

3 December Robert Cantwell interviews Faulkner at Rowan Oak before publishing an article in the 23 January 1939 issue of *Time,* the cover of which features Faulkner as the author of *The Wild Palms.*

15 December Robert Haas receives a long and remarkable letter describing the "Snopes" project in detail. The germ of the trilogy dates back to the winter of 1926–1927, when Faulkner had begun a story entitled "Father Abraham."[98] The three books now planned, Faulkner writes, are to be entitled: THE PEASANTS, RUS IN URBE, ILIUM FALLING. He says he is halfway through volume 1, which "will run about 80,000 words," and of which "three chapters have been printed in mags. as short stories, though not in my collections yet" (*SLWF,* p. 107).[99]

One short story was published in 1938: "An Odor of Verbena" in *The Unvanquished* (15 February).

---

[96] If I forget thee, O Jerusalem, let my right hand forget her cunning, Psalm 137:5.

[97] See facsimile in *LCWF,* figure 15.

[98] *Father Abraham* by William Faulkner was published in a limited edition of 210 copies (New York: Red Ozier Press, 1983) edited by James B. Meriwether, and with wood engravings by John DePol, and in a trade issue (New York: Random House, 1984). The editor concludes his introduction aptly: "The young Faulkner— that is, the writer he was until he wrote *The Sound and the Fury*—did nothing more ambitious, or more successful."

[99] These three are "Spotted Horses" (*Scribner's,* June 1931, pp. 585–97); "Lizards in Jamshyd's Courtyard" (*The Saturday Evening Post,* 27 February 1932, pp. 12ff.); "Fool About a Horse" (*Scribner's,* August 1936, pp. 80–86).

1939   *18 January*   Faulkner is elected to the National Institute of Arts and Letters, with Marjorie Kinnan Rawlings and John Steinbeck. This, along with two essays written by George Marion O'Donnell and Conrad Aiken, published the same year, can be said to mark the beginning of Faulkner's recognition in his own country.[100]

19 January   Publication of *The Wild Palms,* a novel consisting of two stories, "Wild Palms" and "Old Man," the five chapters of one alternating with the five chapters of the other in a way Faulkner himself called "contrapuntal" (*FITU,* p. 171; *LITG,* p. 247).

7 February   Haas receives a letter in which Faulkner claims to have written "215 pages" of a novel (*The Hamlet,* volume 1 of the Snopes trilogy).

March   On this novel Faulkner receives an advance of $1,200, which he uses immediately to pay the debts of his old friend Phil Stone.

End of March   The sales of *The Wild Palms,* more than 1,000 copies per week, surpass those of *Sanctuary.*

5 April   In an interview published in New Orleans, Faulkner reveals that he is "now working on a three-volume novel he began in New Orleans 15 years ago. He'd have finished it sooner, but for boiling the pot. It's about a poor white who comes to a little Southern town and teaches the populace corruption in government . . ." (*LITG,* p. 37).

24 April   Haas receives the corrections for book 1 of *The Hamlet,* with the following handwritten postscript: "I am the best in America, by God" (*SLWF,* p. 113).

May   Faulkner stops work on the novel to write "Hand Upon the Waters," a detective story for which *The Saturday Evening Post* would pay $1,000.

August   After resuming work on his novel, Faulkner tries, in vain, to sign a contract with Hollywood—an unmistakable sign of his financial difficulties.

---

[100] The two essays were George Marion O'Donnell's "Faulkner's Mythology" (*Kenyon Review,* Summer 1939), pp. 285–99, and Conrad Aiken's "William Faulkner: The Novel as Form" (*Atlantic Monthly,* November 1939), pp. 150–54. Both were reprinted in *FACCE* and in *TCH.*

3 October   Harold Ober receives "The Old People," the first (in chronological order of composition)[101] of the series of stories which, after much revision, would eventually constitute *Go Down, Moses* (1942).

24 October   Faulkner writes Vincent Sheean to donate the manuscript of *Absalom, Absalom!* to the cause of the Spanish Loyalists (*FAB,* p. 1030).

October   Saxe Commins receives the last chapter of the first part of the Snopes trilogy, the three parts of which are now to be entitled *The Hamlet, The Town,* and *The Mansion.*

November   Publication of "Hand Upon the Waters," the third of the five stories which, along with the title novella, would eventually become *Knight's Gambit* (1949).

Two stories were published in 1939:

1. "Barn Burning," *Harper's,* 179 (June) pp. 86–96; reprinted in *CSWF.*

2. "Hand Upon the Waters," *The Saturday Evening Post,* 212 (4 November) pp. 14 ff.; reprinted in *Knight's Gambit.*

1940   *4 January*   Ober receives "A Point of Law," later to be published, untitled, as the first chapter of the second part of *Go Down, Moses*; it was sold to *Collier's* for $1,000.

31 January   Caroline Barr dies at Rowan Oak (see *1902*). Faulkner delivers a short funeral sermon, the text of which, sent by him to Robert Haas on 7 February, would be reprinted by James B. Meriwether in 1965 in *ESPL* (pp. 117–18). On the tombstone in the Oxford cemetery are the dates "1840–1940," but Faulkner wrote to Haas on 5 February: "The old lady was about 95" (*SLWF,* p. 117).

February   On 5 February, Faulkner returns the proofs of *The Hamlet* to Haas. On the 19th, Ober receives "Gold Is Not Always," and on the 23d, "The Fire on the Hearth." Along with "A Point of Law," these stories, without their titles, would constitute the three chapters entitled "The Fire and the Hearth," the second part of *Go Down, Moses.*

18 March   Ober receives the story "Pantaloon in Black,"

---

[101] With the exception of "Lion" (see *March* [?] *1935,* and note 115).

which would be placed as the third part of *Go Down, Moses.*

1 April   Publication of *The Hamlet,* the first volume of the Snopes trilogy, which brings together, after considerable revisions, six stories already published or to be published separately: to the three alluded to in Faulkner's letter to Haas on 15 December 1938 (see *note 99*) must be added "Afternoon of a Cow" (see *20–26 June 1937* and *note 93*), "Barn Burning" (see *September–November 1938*), and "The Hound" (see *1931*). The book is dedicated to Phil Stone.

18 and 28 April   Faulkner sends bitter letters to his publisher concerning his financial difficulties. Haas replies that *The Hamlet* has sold 6,780 copies as of April 30 but that Faulkner should not expect to make more than $3,000 on a book. He suggests a plan covering three books, an immediate payment of $1,000, a second of $2,000 the following year, and $250 a month for two years after that.

3 May   Faulkner replies: "Your promptness was kind, your response comforting, your suggestion generous" (*SLWF,* p. 122). He goes on to accept Haas's proposal with a few changes: he will first write a collection of short stories, then a novel whose plot he outlines. In broad terms, it is that of his last novel, *The Reivers* (1962).

It is both characteristic of the mature Faulkner, and probably unique in the history of literature, that his literary creation should thus grow out of two different, almost contradictory "movements." The first is one of haste, or, perhaps a better word, of such "drive" that left him no rest from the completion of one novel to the inception, or even to the actual writing, of another. Such was the case in 1938–1939, when no sooner had *The Wild Palms* been completed than he began work on *The Hamlet.* The second "movement" is one of "mellow fruitfulness" under the "maturing sun" of time. Consider these three examples:

1. "Father Abraham" was written in the winter of 1926–1927, and yet Faulkner did not resume work on his Snopes material until at least ten years after that date.

2. In a letter to Harrison Smith dated October 1933,

Faulkner writes that he has the title and apparently also the "esoteric" topic of *Requiem for a Nun,* which he would not complete until the spring of 1951.

3. *The Reivers* was completed in August 1961, though its substance was the subject of a letter to Robert Haas in May 1940.

It may be possible at this point to generalize tentatively about Faulkner's literary creation in the following way. Whether the original "germ" of a book or of a story was a scene (as André Malraux thought was the case with *Sanctuary* [*FACCE,* p. 272], and as Faulkner himself said was the case with *Light in August* [*FITU,* p. 74]), a character (the "nun" of *Requiem,* or "a sort of Huck Finn—a normal boy of about twelve or thirteen" [*SLWF,* p. 123], the future Lucius Priest of *The Reivers*) or an idea (as seems to have been the case with such an "esoteric" story as "Beyond" or with *A Fable*), Faulkner's imagination can be conceived as working upon it in the way a snowball builds itself—or, to revert to the "organic" metaphor which he was so fond of using, in gestation.

A similar conclusion can be reached if one studies the relationship between novels and stories. It is well-known, since Faulkner said so to Maurice Edgar Coindreau (*TTWF,* p. 41), that *The Sound and the Fury* was "incepted" as a short story. It is likewise as revealing as it is puzzling to see him use the same title, *As I Lay Dying,* for two works, a story and a novel, with nothing in common except the study in dialect; in this case, it may even be said that the title, although borrowed from the *Odyssey,* is the thing wherein we might catch the unconscious of the author. One can also cite the intensely metaphorical nature of the title "Carcassonne," or even Faulkner's extraordinary fidelity to Keats's "Ode on a Grecian Urn," the text of which is subtly woven into more than one novel, from *Light in August* to *Go Down, Moses.*

To put it briefly, Faulkner's work can be seen as paradigmatic for two reasons, or on two grounds at least: the extreme idealism which is coextensive with the repeated compulsion to express verbally one's own psyche, and the busy, ceaseless operation of the shuttle of intertextuality.

55

22 May   Again, Faulkner presses upon Haas the idea already put forth in his letter of 3 May: ". . . Ober has four stories about niggers. I can build onto them, write some more, make a book like *The Unvanquished,* could get it together in six months, perhaps" (*SLWF,* p. 124). [102] The book he describes would be called *Go Down, Moses.* [103]

27 May   In quite a different letter to Haas, Faulkner reveals both another side of his personality and what was perhaps the main reason for his present depression: "What a hell of a time we are facing. I got my uniform out the other day. . . . Of course I could do no good, would last about two minutes in combat. But my feeling now is better so: that what will be left after this one will certainly not be worth living for. Maybe the watching of all this coming to a head for the last year is why I cant write, dont seem to want to write, that is. But I can still write. That is, I haven't said at 42 all that is in the cards for me to say. And that wont do any good either, but surely it is still possible to scratch the face of the supreme Obliteration and leave a decipherable scar of some sort" (*SLWF,* p. 125).

7 June   Since Haas grants him another advance of $2,400 on the proposed collection of stories, Faulkner sends him a three-page letter in which he outlines his financial situation and a list of his literary assets: the projected novel mentioned in April, "5 short stories already written, two others planned, both of which might sell, one of which is a mystery story, original in that the solver is a negro, himself in jail for the murder and is about to be lynched, solves murder in self defense. Of these I can make a more or less continuous narrative, somewhat after THE UNVANQUISHED. 6–12 months." [104] And finally "Four other short stories, unwritten, of the first class, but which I now dare not put any time on because first class stories fetch no money in America." Faulkner boldly concludes with an ultimatum: "So besides the $3,000.00 advance on the new un-

---

[102] See note 115 for a chronological recapitulation of the composition of the novel.
[103] See *4 January, February,* and *18 March 1940.*
[104] The mystery story appears to be the germ of *Intruder in the Dust* (1948). The other stories mentioned in this letter were to be collected under the title *Knight's Gambit.*

written novel, I need $4,000.00 more by Jan. 1. If your judgment forbids you to get more deeply involved, let me take the collected story idea and try to sell it somewhere else for that much advance" (*SLWF*, pp. 127–29).

10 June   Haas, too, draws up a list:

Absalom, Absalom!	brought	in	$3,037
The Unvanquished	"	"	$2,327
The Wild Palms	"	"	$5,360
The Hamlet	"	"	$2,700

Haas decides that these figures do not justify any additional advance and leaves Faulkner free to act. Faulkner, in turn, writes to Harold Guinzburg of Viking Press, who, at the time of the publication of *Sanctuary,* had expressed interest in publishing Faulkner's works. [105] According to Faulkner, Guinzburg had "intimated . . . that I could almost write my own ticket with him" (*SLWF*, p. 129).

18 June   Faulkner cables Random House the news that he has "RECEIVED CONTRACT OFFER FOR SHORT STORY BOOK AND A NOVEL. INFERENCE IS THAT I WILL BE PUBLISHED FROM NOW ON BY NEW FIRM. WOULD LIKE TO HAVE YOUR ACKNOWLEDGEMENT BEFORE CLOSING. WILL WAIT UNTIL NOON WEDNESDAY. WILL COME NEW YORK TO SETTLE DETAILS" (*SLWF*, p. 130).

19 June   Since Robert Haas is out of town, Bennett Cerf, feeling that Faulkner was getting away from Random House, answers both the letter of 7 June and the telegram of 18 June: "All of us are absolutely sick at heart at the thought of your leaving Random House" (*FAB*, p. 1050). He adds $2,000 to the $2,400 Haas has already offered for the short story collection—and he gets in touch with Guinzburg, who would have to pay for the 2,500 unsold copies of *The Hamlet* if he wished to "buy" Faulkner.

3 July   Guinzburg writes that he must withdraw his offer; the purchase of the plates and of the unsold copies of *The Hamlet* amounting to $1,500, to be added to the $6,000 he has pro-

---

[105] See *26 October 1931.*

posed to Faulkner as an advance on his royalties, make the transaction too expensive. Joseph Blotner notes: "Faulkner was almost, though not quite, back where he had started from" (*FAB,* p. 1053).

July   Faulkner revises "Almost"[106] and sends "Go Down, Moses"[107] directly to *The Saturday Evening Post,* which turns it down.

August   *Harper's* buys "Pantaloon in Black"[108] for $400, and *The Saturday Evening Post* pays $1,000 for "Tomorrow."[109]

September   The *Atlantic Monthly* buys "Gold Is Not Always,"[110] and *Collier's* buys "Go Down, Moses."

October   Having "received no call from R.A.F.," Faulkner teaches navigation and radio operation to young volunteers in Mississippi. He is writing nothing "save pot-boilers" (*SLWF,* p. 136).

November   Having sent the detective story "An Error in Chemistry" to Harold Ober, Faulkner goes hunting with his local friends in the "big woods," where he does not "fret and stew so much about Europe" (*SLWF,* p. 138).

December   Ober receives "Delta Autumn."[111]

Five stories were published in 1940:

1. "A Point of Law," *Collier's,* 105 (22 June) pp. 20ff., revised for incorporation in *Go Down, Moses,* where it appears, untitled, as chapter 1 of the second part of the book, "The Fire and the Hearth;" magazine version reprinted in *USWF.*

2. "The Old People," *Harper's,* 181 (September) pp. 418–25; revised for *Go Down, Moses,* part 4; magazine version reprinted in *USWF.*

---

[106] This story, the sixth of the series sent to Harold Ober, would become "Was," the first of the seven parts of *Go Down, Moses.* It was turned down by *The Saturday Evening Post.*

[107] This story, the seventh of the series, would be incorporated under the same title as the last part of the volume with the same title.

[108] See *18 March 1940.*

[109] To be incorporated in *Knight's Gambit.*

[110] See *February 1940.*

[111] This, the eighth story to be received by Ober, would be bought and published by *Story* and become the next-to-the-last part of *Go Down, Moses.*

3. "Pantaloon in Black," *Harper's,* 181 (October) pp. 503–13; revised for *Go Down, Moses,* part 3; magazine version reprinted in *USWF.*

4. "Gold Is Not Always," *Atlantic,* 166 (November) pp. 563–70; revised for *Go Down, Moses,* where it appears, untitled, as chapter 2 of the second part of the book, "The Fire and the Hearth"; magazine version reprinted in *USWF.*

5. "Tomorrow," *Saturday Evening Post,* 213 (23 November) pp. 22ff.; revised in *Knight's Gambit.*

1941 *21 March* Faulkner to Robert Haas: "I am still writing short stories, to finish paying the back income tax" (*SLWF,* pp. 139–40); in fact, he has just sent Ober "The Tall Men," which would be published by *The Saturday Evening Post* on 31 May.

May Faulkner resumes work on *Go Down, Moses,* the "general theme" of which is the "relationship between white and negro races here" (*SLWF,* p. 139). However, at this stage, he writes about the book as being "about the size and similar to *The Unvanquished.*" Thus, it is clear that he is not yet thinking of "The Bear." Meanwhile, a new agent, William Herndon, is trying in vain to find Faulkner a contract in Hollywood.

5 June Chapter 1 of "The Fire and the Hearth"—a new version of the story "A Point of Law," is received by Haas.

18 June Ben Wasson, accompanied by Shelby Foote,[112] visits Faulkner, who seems to have now interrupted his revision of the stories and to have begun work on "The Bear."

July Faulkner is now well along in the writing of *Go Down, Moses,* which, in his mind, would not be a simple collection of stories, but a united group of revised texts forming a single work. After finishing "The Old People," he begins "Delta Autumn" on page 186 of his typescript and continues until page 200, at which point he introduces the beginning of "The Bear," to be inserted between the two preceding parts.

---

[112] At the time, Shelby Foote had written half a dozen short stories. He later wrote five novels and *The Civil War: A Narrative* (1958, 1963, 1974). For Faulkner's opinion of him in 1957, see *FITU,* p. 50.

6 July Faulkner writes a letter to Warren Beck approving the articles which Professor Beck had published about his work (*SLWF*, pp. 142–43).[113]

25 July Faulkner sends Haas the first chapter of "The Bear" (which ends on page 206 in his typescript), and begins the second; at this point, he is going to use the story entitled "Lion" which he had published in 1935.[114]

9 September Haas receives the typescript of the second chapter of "The Bear."

27 October Harold Ober receives a short story entitled "The Bear" that is meant for a magazine—and for money. It is a much shorter version (*without* chapter 4, which has not been written yet).

9 November Chapter 3 of "The Bear" (*Go Down, Moses* version) received by Haas.

14 November After Faulkner has agreed to revise the ending of the short story "The Bear," which had been offered to several magazines toward the end of October, *The Saturday Evening Post* buys it for $1,000.

2 December Faulkner to Haas: "My promise re mss. Dec 1 is already broken. There is more meat in it than I thought, a section now that I am going to be proud of and which requires careful writing and rewriting to get it exactly right. I am at it steadily. . . ." (*SLWF*, p. 146). This would be the fourth chapter of "The Bear" in the *Go Down, Moses* version.

Mid-December Saxe Commins, the author's new editor at Random House, receives one hundred twenty-one typewritten pages along with a note containing firm instructions to the printer: "DON'T CHANGE EITHER THE PUNCTUATION OR THE CONSTRUCTION." Then, Faulkner expands the first version of "Delta Autumn" in order to adapt it to the book. In sending it,

---

[113] "Faulkner and the South," *Antioch Review*, 1 (March 1941), 82–94; "Faulkner's Point of View," *College English*, 2 (May 1941), 736–49; "William Faulkner's Style," *American Prefaces*, 4 (Spring 1941), 195–211; all three were reprinted in *Faulkner: Essays by Warren Beck* (Madison: University of Wisconsin Press, 1976).

[114] Beginning with this date (25 July 1941), it is important to distinguish between two separate uses of the same texts: the *short stories* Faulkner sent to Harold Ober for magazines, and for money, and the *parts* he sent to Robert Haas in view of the publication of the *book*.

he asks Saxe Commins to add the story "Go Down, Moses" and to use its title as the title of the now-completed volume.

Two stories were published in 1941:
    1. "Go Down, Moses," *Collier's,* 107 (25 January) pp. 19ff.; revised to be the seventh and last chapter of *Go Down, Moses;* magazine version reprinted in *USWF.*
    2. "The Tall Men," *The Saturday Evening Post,* 213 (31 May) pp. 14ff.; reprinted in *CSWF.*

1942   *21 January*   Faulkner sends Robert Haas the text of the dedication to be published in *Go Down, Moses:*

To Mammy
CAROLINE BARR
Mississippi
[1840–1940]
Who was born in slavery and who
gave to my family a fidelity without
stint or calculation of recompense
and to my childhood an immeasur-
able devotion and love.

9 May   Publication of the short story of "The Bear" in *The Saturday Evening Post.*

11 May   Publication of *Go Down, Moses and Other Stories.* For the second edition of the book (see *26 January 1949*), Faulkner has the words "and other stories" deleted thus emphasizing the unity of the work. "Moses is indeed a novel," he would write to Haas on 26 January 1949 (see that date). The book is made up of seven texts or "parts," several of which, like "Was," appear for the first time, while others are revisions of one or even several stories already published or unpublished (such as "The Fire on the Hearth").[115] The success of the book is not con-

---

[115] Listed below, in the order in which they appear in the book, are the seven texts which make up *Go Down, Moses.* As Faulkner usually addressed them first to Harold Ober Associates, I provide, in parentheses, the date on which each was received, the title that Faulkner had chosen for its publication in a magazine, and for those which were actually published as short stories, the magazine, date, and variant title:
    I. "Was" (received 1 July 1940 under the title "Almost").
    II. "The Fire and the Hearth":
        1. First chapter (received on 4 January 1940 under the title "A Point of

siderable, with the notable exception of its fifth part, "The Bear," which would be hailed as one of the summits of Faulkner's art. [116]

Meanwhile, Faulkner experiences great financial difficulty: for the entire year 1942, the royalties paid to him by Random House do not exceed $300. It is therefore easy to understand why, during the spring, he multiplies his letters to Harold Ober requesting that he either try and sell short stories or obtain a new contract in Hollywood. [117]

17 July   Ober receives "Shingles for the Lord," the seventh

Law" and published in *Collier's,* 105, 22 June 1940, pp. 20ff.).
2. Second chapter (received on 19 February 1940 under the title "Gold Is Not Always" and published in *Atlantic,* 166, November 1940, pp. 563–70).
3. Third chapter (received on 23 February 1940 under the title "The Fire on the Hearth").
III. "Pantaloon in Black" (received on 18 March 1940 and published in *Harper's,* 181, October 1940, pp. 503–13).
IV. "The Old People" (received on 3 October 1939 and published in *Harper's,* 181, September 1940, pp. 418–25).
V. "The Bear":
1. The short story entitled "Lion" (received by Morton Goldman in March [?] 1935 and published in *Harper's,* 172, December 1935, pp. 67–77). This constitutes the germ from which the fifth part of *Go Down, Moses* was written between July and December 1941.
2. The story entitled "The Bear" (received on 27 October 1941 and published in *The Saturday Evening Post,* 214, 9 May 1942, pp. 30ff., two days before the publication of the novel) was "taken from the chapter by that name" (letter to Saxe Commins, probably mid-December 1941, *SLWF,* p. 147).
VI. "Delta Autumn" (received on 16 December 1940 and published in *Story,* 20, May–June 1942, pp. 46–55).
VII. "Go Down, Moses" (received 1 August 1940 and published in *Collier's,* 107 25 January 1941, pp. 19ff.).
[116] Unfortunately, since Faulkner always insisted that if anyone wished to read the story separately, it would be best to leave out chapter 4, which indeed is the axis of the book, not of the story: see *FIU,* pp. 4, 273, and *LIG,* p. 59. On "The Bear," see in particular *Bear, Man, and God: Seven Approaches to William Faulkner's "The Bear",* ed. F. L. Utley, L. Z. Bloom, and A. F. Kinney (New York: Random House, 1964). An expanded edition entitled *Eight Approaches* was published in 1971.
[117] "I am trying to raise $1,000.00. . . . I have touched bottom . . . The trouble is, I cant sell stories. Wrote 6 since Jan., sold one." Letter to Bennett Cerf, probably 23 June 1942 (*SLWF,* p. 154).

story Faulkner has sent him since the beginning of the year. On 28 July, he sells it for $1,000 to *The Saturday Evening Post.*

27 July   After a stormy argument about a contract, Faulkner arrives in Burbank, California, for his eighth stint with the film industry. He hopes for a year's contract with Warner Bros. but has to sign for seven years (only a formality, he is told) at $300 a week—less than what he received as a novice with MGM, ten years before.[118] This contract would become a nightmare for Faulkner, and one can well believe that the situation is painful, if not humiliating, for one who has just reached, with his thirteenth novel, a high point in American literature.

3 August   Faulkner is given as a first assignment the editing of "The De Gaulle Story."

15 September   Henry Miller notes that Faulkner "only gets three hundred a week at Warner Brothers Studio."[119]

October   Faulkner meets Ruth Ford, a former student at the University of Mississippi and now an actress also under contract to Warner Bros.

16 November   Faulkner, interested in the subject, has written 153 pages of "The De Gaulle Story." The film, however, is never produced, perhaps for political reasons: Roosevelt allegedly did not like the idea of praising De Gaulle at the expense of Churchill (see *FAB,* p. 1130).

December   Faulkner enjoys a "furlough" for a month and spends Christmas with his family. Shortly before leaving Los Angeles, he writes to his stepson, Malcolm Franklin: "There is something here for an anthropologist's notebook. This is one of the richest towns in the country. As it exists today, its economy and geography was fixed and invented by the automobile. Therefore, the automobile invented it. The automobile (for a time, anyway) is as dead as the mastodon. Therefore the town which the automobile created, is dying" (*SLWF,* p. 166). Even though Random House would help Faulkner get out of his contract later on, the period beginning on 27 July 1942 and ending on 21 September 1945 (the date on which he was finally released from his contract) would be, in spite of the "fur-

---

[118] See 7 *May–26 June 1932.*
[119] Letter to Lawrence Durrell quoted in *FAB,* p. 155n.

loughs,"[120] his longest and most laborious stint in Hollywood. He worked on no fewer than seventeen scripts (see *FIH*, pp. 280–96).

Three short stories were published in 1942:

1. "Two Soldiers," *The Saturday Evening Post*, 214 (28 March) pp. 9ff.; reprinted in *CSWF*.

2. "The Bear," *The Saturday Evening Post*, 214 (9 May), pp. 30ff.; drawn from the fifth part of *Go Down, Moses;* reprinted in *USWF*.

3. "Delta Autumn," *Story*, 20 (May–June) pp. 46–55; revised for *Go Down, Moses*; part of this version used for the ending of *Big Woods* (1955); magazine version reprinted in *USWF*.

1943 *16 January* Faulkner, in Hollywood again, works on *Northern Pursuit,* a derring-do script written for Errol Flynn.

13 February After "Shingles for the Lord" is published in *The Saturday Evening Post,* Faulkner will not publish more than six stories during the next twelve and a half years (until October 1955).

March Faulkner works on *Deep Valley,* a script somewhat reminiscent of the part entitled "Old Man" in *The Wild Palms.* Faulkner then works on *Country Lawyer,* in which, according to Joseph Blotner, he includes some aspects of his own imaginary universe. The film was never produced.

April Faulkner still hopes either to enter military service or to return to Oxford to take care of his farm. He writes on 3 April to William Fielden, his stepdaughter's husband, that he has "the damned worst bloody rotten bad cold in human captivity" (*SLWF*, p. 169)—a rare outburst in his correspondence.

Spring After working on *Battle Cry* with Howard Hawks, Faulkner is assigned to *To Have and Have Not,* based on the novel Hawks had persuaded his friend Hemingway to sell to Hollywood. However, Faulkner does not work on the screenplay until after his return from the vacation granted him by Warner's, theoretically until 15 November, but which, in fact, lasted until mid-February 1944.

As Blotner notes, Faulkner has undertaken "a project that

---

[120] These were the periods during which, as he wrote to Ober on 25 May 1945, his contract was "simply suspended" (*SLWF*, p. 192).

would be far more complicated and protracted than he could imagine" (*FIH*, p. 288; *FAB*, p. 1150). The idea comes from director Henry Hathaway, at the time associated with William Bacher, the producer. The plot is to revolve around a reincarnation of Christ during the First World War, and this sacrificial avatar is to merge with that of the Unknown Soldier buried under the Arc de Triomphe in Paris. Only Faulkner could write that, they said—and, as incredible as it may sound, Faulkner is influenced by their enthusiasm. It is agreed that the three of them would produce the film independently. Bacher begins by lending $1,000 to Faulkner who, after obtaining a leave from Warner Bros., returns home to begin work (mid-August). According to the contract he has signed, however, Faulkner owes Warner Bros. the exclusive rights for his work on the script, so he sets to writing it in his own fashion, ready to transform it into a script after the contract expires.

30 October From Rowan Oak, Faulkner writes to Harold Ober: "I am working on a thing now. It will be about 10–15 thousand words. It is a fable, an indictment of war perhaps, and for that reason may not be acceptable now" (*SLWF*, p. 178). At this stage, the work is tentatively entitled "Who?"

Mid-November Faulkner sends Ober a first version of his work-in-progress in the form of a 51-page "treatment" (*FAF*, p. 174), a copy of which is also sent to Bacher and Hathaway.

Besides "L'Après-Midi d'une Vache," Maurice Edgar Coindreau's translation of the typescript of "Afternoon of a Cow" which Faulkner had given him in 1937 and which was published before the original in *Fontaine* (Algiers) under the pseudonym "Ernest V. Trueblood," three other stories were published in 1943:

1. "Shingles for the Lord," *The Saturday Evening Post*, 215 (13 February) pp. 14ff.; reprinted in *CSWF*.

2. "My Grandmother Millard and General Bedford Forrest and the Battle of Harrykin Creek," *Story*, 22 (March–April) pp. 68–86; reprinted in *CSWF*.

3. "Shall Not Perish," *Story*, 23 (July–August) pp. 40–47; reprinted in *CSWF*.

1944 *8 January* Faulkner writes to Ober: "I have finished the first draft of the fable, and have started rewriting it. I go back to Cal. 10th February, hope to finish rewriting it by then" (*SLWF*, p. 179.)

14 February   Upon his return to Hollywood, Faulkner must drop his fable in order to begin work on *To Have and Have Not*, which keeps him busy for two months.

7 May   Faulkner's first reply to Malcolm Cowley, who was then completing *The Portable Hemingway* for Viking Press and who wanted material to write an article on Faulkner, reveals Faulkner's sense of privacy: "I would like the piece, except the biography part" (*SLWF*, p. 182; *TFCF*, p. 7). In the same letter, for the first time, he uses the phrase "the salt mines" to describe his work in Hollywood.

24 June–7 September   Estelle and Jill join Faulkner in Hollywood.

28 August   Writing for Hawks again, Faulkner begins the adaptation of Raymond Chandler's *The Big Sleep* for Warner Bros.[121]

29 October   Publication in the *New York Times Book Review* of Malcolm Cowley's "William Faulkner's Human Comedy." Cowley would write in 1966: "The public, which had been briefly excited by *Sanctuary* in 1931, had ceased to read Faulkner's work. . . . His seventeen books were effectively out of print and seemed likely to remain in that condition, since there was no public demand for them. How could one speak of Faulkner's value on the literary stock exchange? In 1944 his name wasn't even listed there" (*TFCF*, p. 5).[122]

December   On the train en route to Oxford, Faulkner dates his last revisions of the script of *The Big Sleep*.

15 December   Back in Oxford, Faulkner finishes the revision of the script, then goes back to work on his "fable."

20 December   Harold Ober forwards an offer from Doubleday

---

[121] "To Faulkner, Dashiell Hammett and Raymond Chandler were the outstanding practitioners of the form [of murder mysteries]." See *FIH*, p. 291.

[122] On 9 August 1945, however, Malcolm Cowley would write to Faulkner: "But the reason the book [*The Portable*] pleases me is that it gives me a chance to present your work as a whole, at a time when every one of your books except "Sanctuary"— and I am not even sure about that—is out of print. The result should be a better sale for your new books and a bayonet prick in the ass of Random House to reprint the others" (*TFCF*, p. 22). Cowley's expectations were realized.

for a book on the Mississippi River that might save Faulkner from Hollywood by guaranteeing him an advance of $5,000. Faulkner, both touched and thankful, replies: "I will write you about the Mississippi River book as soon as I get my breath. I like the idea very much. That is, I am grateful to the blokes who thought of it, very pleased and comforted that such men exist, not just on my account but for the sake of writing, art, and artists, in America and the world. The reason I dont seem yet to know my own mind on the subject is as follows:

I have never done a book of that sort, never had the notion to do one, and so I dont know exactly where to begin. So in a sense that means to learn a new trade at age of 47 (assuming that for me to do such a book will be tour de force[123]), starting 'cold,' without that speck of fire, that coal, from which a book or a picture should burst almost of its own accord. I am 47. I have 3 more books of my own I want to write. I am like an aging mare, who has say three more gestations in her before her time is over, and doesn't want to spend one of them breeding what she considers (wrongly perhaps) a mule.

So let me think about it a little longer. . . . " (*SLWF*, p. 187).

1945 *January* Random House agrees to advance $2,000 or $3,000 to Faulkner, and he finally decides against Doubleday's offer.

20 January Premiere of the film *To Have and Have Not*, produced and directed by Howard Hawks. Faulkner's name appears in the credits.

19 March Faulkner writes to Ober: "It will take some time yet to finish the mss [*A Fable*]. It may be my epic poem" (*SLWF*, p. 191).

June Faulkner is back in Hollywood for his eleventh and last stint. He begins work on Stephen Longstreet's *Stallion Road*, but it is withdrawn from him. He then collaborates with Jean

---

[123] For other uses of the same French expression (which Faulkner probably used in the first of the two senses given by Webster: 1. A feat of strength, skill, or artistic merit. 2. A merely adroit or ingenious accomplishment or production), see *FIU*, pp. 60 ("The Bear"), 113, 207 *(As I Lay Dying)*.

Renoir on the final screenplay of *The Southerner*. He also works on *A Fable*.

20 August   Still attempting to free himself from his oppressive seven-year contract, Faulkner writes to Ober: "I think I have had about all of Hollywood I can stand (*SLWF*, p. 199).

9 August   "Pour les jeunes en France, Faulkner c'est un dieu" (For the young people in France, Faulkner is a god). Malcolm Cowley attributes these words to Jean-Paul Sartre (*TFCF*, p. 24). One can easily imagine how bitterly ironic this news must have been to one who was toiling for $500 a week in the "salt mines."

5 October   "Yes, I had become aware of Faulkner's European reputation. The night before I left Hollywood [in September] I went (under pressure) to a party. I was sitting on a sofa with a drink, suddenly realised I was being pretty intently listened to by three men whom I then realised were squatting on their heels and knees in a kind of circle in front of me. They were Isherwood, the English poet and a French surrealist, Hélion; the other's name I forget." Faulkner to Cowley (*TFCF*, p. 35; *SLWF*, p. 203).

10 August   Premiere of Jean Renoir's film *The Southerner*. Although Faulkner's name does not appear in the credits because of contractual obligations, it is, according to Malcolm Cowley, the film Faulkner considered as "his best picture" (*TFCF*, p. 106).

11 September   Though he prefers *Native Son* (1940), Faulkner writes to Richard Wright concerning the recent publication of *Black Boy*: "I think that you will agree that the good lasting stuff comes out of one individual's imagination and sensitivity to and comprehension of the suffering of Everyman, Anyman, not out of the memory of his own grief" (*SLWF*, p. 201).

18 October   Back at Rowan Oak, Faulkner sends to Cowley the "synopsis," or the "induction" (*SLWF*, p. 204) which he has been writing for Cowley to "introduce" the excerpt from *The Sound and the Fury* in the *The Portable Faulkner*. It turns out to be what is now called the "Compson Appendix."[124]

---

[124] For an evaluation and history of this important piece, see James B.

Winter 1945–1946 Faulkner tries again and again to free himself legally from his contract, but Warner Bros. is determined to declare itself the owner of all that Faulkner writes since he signed the contract. "So Faulkner wont do any writing until he finds out just how much of his soul he no longer owns," Faulker writes to Robert Haas on 2 November (*SLWF*, p. 210).

8 December Faulkner sends to Cowley, who had been pressing him for it, an important autobiographical letter that I have mentioned several times. It is preceded by the following statement about Cowley's work-in-progress, *The Portable Faulkner*: "It's not a new work by Faulkner. It's a new work by Cowley all right though" (*SLWF*, p. 211; *TFCF*, p. 66).

24 December In Cowley's introduction to *The Portable Faulkner*, Faulkner corrects a statement regarding his war record: "When the war was over—the other war—William Faulkner, at home again in Oxford, Mississippi, yet at the same time was not at home, or at least not able to accept the postwar world" (*SLWF*, p. 213; *TFCF*, p. 74). Cowley comments: "Why didn't he say flatly that he hadn't served in France during the war?" (*TFCF*, p. 65). So he writes again to Faulkner on this subject.

1946 *Beginning of January* Faulkner writes to Cowley: "If you mention military experience at all (which is not necessary, as I could have invented a few failed RAF airmen as easily as I did Confeds) say 'belonged to RAF in 1918'" (*SLWF*, p. 215; *TFCF*, p. 77).

5 January Faulkner to Harold Ober: "Thank you for the Ellery Queen check. What a commentary. In France, I am the father of a literary movement. In Europe I am considered the best modern American and among the first of all writers. In America, I eke out a hack's motion picture wages by winning second prize in a manufactured mystery story contest." ("An

---

Meriwether's "The Textual History of *The Sound and the Fury*" in *Studies in "The Sound and the Fury*," comp. by James B. Meriwether (Columbus, Ohio: Charles E. Merrill, 1970), pp. 1–32.

Error in Chemistry" had won second prize in a detective story contest organized by *Ellery Queen's Mystery Magazine.*) Faulkner adds something which tells his real feelings about *The Portable Faulkner*: "Malcolm Cowley has done a fine job in Spoonrivering my apocryphal county . . ." (*SLWF*, pp. 217–18).[125]

21 January Cowley still finds it "hard to believe that his vivid stories about aviators in France—"Ad Astra," "Turnabout," "All the Dead Pilots"—and his portraits of spiritually maimed veterans, living corpses, in *Soldiers' Pay* and *Sartoris* were based on anything but direct experience" (*TFCF*, p. 72). So Faulkner has to repeat his noncommittal and strictly objective formulation: "Was a member of the RAF in 1918." He adds, however: "I'll pay for any resetting of type, plates, alteration, etc." (*TFCF*, p. 82; *SLWF*, p. 219). Cowley finally understands, and Faulkner replies on 1 February: "I don't like the paragraph because it makes me more of a hero than I was" (*TFCF*, pp. 83–84; *SLWF*, p. 219).[126]

4 February To Robert Linscott, a new editor at Random House, who is considering republishing *The Sound and the Fury* and *As I Lay Dying* in a single volume, Faulkner recommends that he take the piece he has written for *The Portable Faulkner,* the "Compson Appendix," and place it "first," in spite of the title, which he wanted retained.[127]

---

[125] *Spoon River Anthology* (1915) is Edgar Lee Masters's outstanding work; it is a series of first-person narratives in verse in which the epitaphs on the tombs in the cemetery of a small, mid-western town are used as a way for each dead inhabitant to tell the story of his life.

[126] "In my search for dependable information I had turned to a useful reference work, *Twentieth Century Authors* (1942). It was edited by Stanley J. Kunitz and Howard Haycraft with some concern for accuracy, in a field where legends abound, but the conflicting stories about Faulkner had proved too much for them. For example, their account of his wartime activities is a short paragraph containing—as I afterward learned—at least five misstatements of fact. It reads: 'The First World War woke him from his lethargy. Flying caught his imagination, but he refused to enlist with the "Yankees," so went to Toronto and joined the Canadian Air Force, becoming a lieutenant in the R.A.F. Biographers who say he got no nearer France than Toronto are mistaken. He was sent to France as an observer, had two planes shot down under him, was wounded in the second shooting, and did not return to Oxford until after the Armistice.' I wanted to accept that paragraph because I had come to think of Faulkner, perhaps rightly, as being among the "wounded writers" of his generation, with Hemingway and others" (*TFCF*, pp. 71–72).

[127] The Compson Appendix would appear at this place in the Modern Library

13 March   Faulkner sends a copy of the "Compson Appendix" to Linscott with a letter stating "it is actually an appendix, not a foreword" (*SLWF*, p. 228).

23 March   The problem of the California contract is solved at last: Warner Bros. will let him finish his novel and disclaims rights to it. The idea is that he will go back to the coast and fulfill the contract when he finishes the novel.[128] Meanwhile, Random House continues to provide a monthly advance on royalties so that Faulkner can stay in Oxford and work. The financial strain will be further eased in late October, when Faulkner spends four weeks working on a script. For the rest of the year and on through 1947 he concentrates on *A Fable* (*FIH*, p. 298).

23 April   Faulkner receives his copy of *The Portable Faulkner* and writes to Cowley: "The job is splendid. Damn you to hell anyway. But even if I had beat you to the idea, mine wouldn't have been this good. By God, I didn't know myself what I had tried to do, and how much I had succeeded." And he adds, with a typically humorous sense of the apt metaphor: "Random House and Ober lit a fire under Warner, I dont know how, and I am here until September anyway, on a dole from Random House, working at what seems now to me to be my magnum o" (*TFCF*, pp. 90–91; *SLWF*, p. 233).

29 April   Publication of *The Portable Faulkner* by Viking Press in New York.[129] Faulkner inscribes a copy for Cowley: "To

---

edition of the novel, see *20 December 1946*. This was the second publication (with variants) of the text. The first was in *The Portable Faulkner*, where it came last in the volume as the latest addition to Faulkner's work.

[128] Faulkner never went back after 2 August 1954, when *A Fable* was published.

[129] In addition to Cowley's introduction and the "Compson Appendix," *The Portable Faulkner* contains:

  I. *The Old People*
      1820.   "A Justice" (from *These 13*)
      1833.   Wedding in the Rain (chapter 2 of *Absalom, Absalom!*)
      18—.   "Red Leaves" (from *These 13*)
      1859.   "Was" (from *Go Down, Moses*)
  II. *The Unvanquished*
      1864.   "Raid" (from *The Unvanquished*)
      1869.   "Wash" (from *Doctor Martino*)
      1874.   "An Odor of Verbena" (from *The Unvanquished*)
  III. *The Last Wilderness*
      1883.   "The Bear" (from *Go Down, Moses*, including chapter 4)

Malcolm Cowley, Who beat me to what was to have been the leisurely pleasure of my old age."

May After "two damned Swedes"[130] whom Faulkner had to see in Rowan Oak on 2 March and who, according to Cowley (*TFCF,* p. 96; *FAB,* p. 1207), had heard Faulkner's name mentioned in relation to the Nobel Prize (which, Cowley cor-

---

IV. *The Peasants*
    1900. Spotted Horses (from *The Hamlet,* chapter 4, part 1)
V. *The End of an Order*
    1902. "That Evening Sun" (from *These 13*)
    1918. "Ad Astra" (from *These 13*)
    1924. "A Rose for Emily" (from *These 13*)
    1928. "Dilsey" (from section 4 of *The Sound and the Fury*)
VI. *Mississippi Flood*
    1927. "Old Man" (one of the sections of *The Wild Palms*)
VII. *Modern Times*
    1928. "Death Drag" (from *Doctor Martino*)
    1929. "Uncle Bud and the Three Madams" (chapter 25 of *Sanctuary*)
    1930. "Percy Grimm" (from chapter 19 of *Light in August*)
    1940. "Delta Autumn" (from *Go Down, Moses*)

This table of contents makes it quite clear that Malcolm Cowley's aim had been to organize Faulkner's works as if they had been conceived methodically, according to the format (both geographical and historical) of a chronicle. Cowley's favorite concept was that of a "Saga," a word that Faulkner himself used only once, in his letter to Cowley dated 8 December 1945, in which he suggests the following description:

  . . . saga of . . . county . . .
A chronological picture of Faulkner's apocryphal
Mississippi county, selected from his published
works, novels and stories, with a heretofore
unpublished genealogy of one of its principal
families (*TFCF,* p. 65; *SLWF,* p. 211).

The description on the front cover of the book reads:

The saga of Yoknapatawpha county, 1820–1945,
Being the first chronological picture of
Faulkner's mythical county in Mississippi. . . .
In effect a new work, though selected from
His best published novels and stories; with
His own account of one of the principal
Families, written especially for this volume.
Edited with an introduction by Malcolm Cowley.

[130] They were Thorsten Jonsson, a reporter for the *Dagens Nyheter* and one of the first translators of Faulkner into Swedish, and his traveling companion (*FAB,* p. 1207).

rectly infers, says a great deal about "the disproportion between Faulkner's American and his European reputation." Faulkner refuses to receive a foreign guest, "this one that cant even speak english" (*TECF*, p. 96; *SLWF*, p. 234; *FAB*, p. 1217). It was the Russian, Ilya Ehrenburg.

5 May Faulkner sends to Robert Haas "a batch" of newly written pages of the work-in-progress: "The central idea has not changed, it just has more in it than I knew at first" (*SLWF*, pp. 233–34).

End of May In a letter to Linscott regarding the use of "Compson Appendix" in the projected edition of *The Sound and the Fury* and *As I Lay Dying*, Faulkner points out that Cowley, in his *Portable*, was wrong in entitling it *"The* Compsons," when it should be "Compson / 1699–1945." Faulkner adds: "Because it's really an obituary, not a segregation" (*SLWF*, p. 237).

July Harold Ober negotiates the sale of film rights to two short stories, "Death Drag" and "Honor," which earns Faulkner $6,600.

31 August Premiere of the film *The Big Sleep* by Howard Hawks, with Humphrey Bogart and Lauren Bacall. Faulkner's name appears in the credits.

October Faulkner sets *A Fable* aside in order to edit a script for $3,500.

November World War II seems to have put an end to Faulkner's passion for flying, and he now takes part in the (52d) annual hunt with his Oxford friends. He misses shooting a fine stag, which he describes in a letter to Robert Haas (*SWLF*, p. 244).

December From Rowan Oak, Faulkner writes to Malcolm Cowley: "It's a dull life here. I need some new people, above all probably a new young woman. But if I leave here I will spend in two weeks money I can live here for two months on, and then I'd have to go back to Cal. At 30 you become aware suddenly that you have become a slave of vast and growing mass of inanimate junk, possessions. . . . Then one day you are almost 50 and you know you never will [escape from it]" (*SLWF*, p. 245).

20 December   Publication in one volume of the Modern Library edition of *The Sound and the Fury* and *As I Lay Dying*, preceded by the "Compson Appendix."

One short story was published in 1946:
    "An Error in Chemistry, *Ellery Queen's Mystery Magazine,* 7 (June) pp. 4–19; reprinted in *Knight's Gambit.*

1947   Faulkner is working on *A Fable.* In July, he writes to Ober that he has finished 400 pages and that he now foresees that it will be about 1,000 pages (*SLWF,* p. 252). In March, he writes a letter to the Oxford newspaper in support of those persons trying to preserve the old courthouse on the square. He is afraid, however, that the cause may already be lost: "They call this progress. But they don't say where it's going; also there are some of us who would like the chance to say whether or not we want the ride" (*ESPL,* p. 203).

From 14 April to 17 April, at the request of the English department at the University of Mississippi, Faulkner agrees to meet with students and answer their questions. One of these, R. M. Allen, "took notes which were later copied and used by other students and by the English Department in preparing an account, for publicity purposes, of the Faulkner class sessions." However, in *The Western Review* 15 (Summer 1951), one of the other students publishes, as "An Interview with William Faulkner" a series of questions and answers from those class sessions, and "a good deal of misunderstanding" is caused by the differences in the two versions of Faulkner's "famous listing of his contemporaries in order of excellence" (*LITG,* pp. 52–53). In the Allen version, which is reprinted in *Lion in the Garden* as being apparently "the most reliable version," Faulkner's answer to the question "Who do you consider the five most important contemporaries?" is: "1. Thomas Wolfe; 2. Dos Passos; 3. Hemingway; 4. Cather [the other version said Caldwell]; 5. Steinbeck. (To the above questioner, a teacher auditing the class turned and added after the above listing, 'I am afraid you are taxing Mr. Faulkner's modesty.' Mr. Faulkner then listed them this way:) 1. Thomas Wolfe—

he had much courage, wrote as if he didn't have long to live. 2. William Faulkner. 3. Dos Passos. 4. Hemingway—he has no courage, has never climbed out on a limb. He has never used a word where the reader might check his usage by a dictionary. 5. Steinbeck—I had great hopes for him at one time. Now I don't know" (*LITG,* p. 58).

There is no exchange of letters between Faulkner and Cowley during 1947, but the correspondence with agent Harold Ober and with editor Saxe Commins testifies to the great toll the writing of *A Fable* is taking on Faulkner and to his growing doubts about his capacities as a writer of fiction.

In the fall, *The Partisan Review* offers to buy an excerpt from the work-in-progress for $1,000. The story of the stolen racehorse appears to be too long, however, and the idea is dropped.[131]

One short story was published in 1947:
"Afternoon of a Cow," *Furioso,* 2 (Summer) pp. 5–17; first published in a French translation by Coindreau in *Fontaine,* 27–28 (June–July 1943); incorporated in *The Hamlet,* chapter 3, part 2; magazine version reprinted in *USWF.*

1948 **15 *January*** Faulkner puts *A Fable* aside to take up a work which he considers to be a detective story, the idea for which goes back to June 1940. He writes *Intruder in the Dust* in three months.

20 April Faulkner sends his manuscript to Robert Haas and, rather suprisingly, asks for his advice about the title. Faulkner holds onto "in the Dust" but is still searching for the first word: "Jugglery," "Impostor," "Intruder"? (*SLWF,* pp. 265–66). On 28 April, he chooses the last one and confirms his choice in a letter to Bennett Cerf in May.

1 June Albert Erskine reads the manuscript, and *Intruder in the Dust* is typeset. (Erskine had recently joined Random House as Saxe Commins's assistant.)

11 July MGM buys film rights to the new novel for $50,000, 20 percent of which is to go to Random House for negotiating the deal.

---

[131] See *February 1951.*

August Faulkner takes up sailing on Sardis Reservoir, formed as the result of a dam recently constructed near Oxford. He even builds his own boat.

15 September Faulkner is in New Orleans to try to obtain a tax reduction. On 18 September, he writes to Haas that he has secured it.

End of September or beginning of October Upon Haas's suggestion that Random House bring out a new collection of Faulkner's short stories, Faulkner reviews each of the titles suggested by Haas (*SLWF*, pp. 274–75).

18 October Faulkner is in New York for the publication of *Intruder in the Dust*. The racial issue in the novel causes repercussions. He sees Ruth Ford again (see *October 1942*). At the Haases', he meets Malcolm Cowley for the first time. Then, alone in his hotel room, he gets drunk and has to be helped. On 23 October, Cowley, who has taken Faulkner to his home in Connecticut, writes in his notebook: "Faulkner is a very small man (5 ft. 5, I should judge), very neatly put together, slim and muscular. Small, beautifully shaped hands. His face has an expression like Poe's in photographs, crooked and melancholy. But his forehead is low, his nose Roman, and his gray hair forms a low wreath around his forehead, so that he also looks like a Roman emperor."

25 October Again, from Cowley's notebook: "Faulkner is 51 years old, weighs 148 pounds, and his waist is so slim that he can wear Robbie's old pants. [Robbie, then in his first year at boarding school, is thirteen and has outgrown the pants.] A small head, very dark brown eyes. One eyebrow goes up, the other down, and perhaps this is what gives him the resemblance to Poe. Hair lies close to his head and is ringleted like a Roman gentleman's" (*TFCF*, pp. 103–05).

1 November Back in Oxford, Faulkner writes to Cowley that he is more and more attracted to the idea of a collection of forty-two short stories arranged according to themes, and he includes an outline of the table of contents which would be that of the *Collected Stories* (1950) (*TFCF*, pp. 116–17; *SLWF*, pp. 278–79). A few weeks later, however, he writes to Saxe Commins: "Ever since I got home I have been thinking about our collected volume. Something nagged at my mind. I have decided (or admitted) that what I seem to be hottest on now, would like first, is another volume. Maybe we are too previous with a collected Faulkner." And he goes on to explain that he is "thinking of a 'Gavin Stevens' volume, more or less detective stories [this would be *Knight's Gambit*]" (*SLWF*, p. 280).

23 November   Faulkner goes deer hunting.

24 November   Faulkner's election to the American Academy of Arts and Letters is announced in the *New York Times*.

One short story was published in 1948:
   "A Courtship," *The Sewanee Review*, 56 (Autumn) pp. 634–53; reprinted in *CSWF*.

1949   During this year, the plans to reprint *The Wild Palms, The Hamlet,* and *Go Down, Moses* are realized.

26 January   With regard to the republication of *Go Down, Moses*, Faulkner writes to Haas: "Moses is indeed a novel. I would not eliminate the story or section titles. Do you think it necessary to number these stories like chapters? Why not reprint exactly, but change the title from GO DOWN, MOSES and other stories, to simply: GO DOWN, MOSES, with whatever change is necessary in the jacket description. We did THE UNVANQUISHED in this manner, without either confusion or anticipation of such; and, for that matter, THE WILD PALMS had two completely unrelated stories in it. Yet nobody thought it should be titled THE WILD PALMS and another story. Indeed, if you will permit me to say so at this late date, nobody but Random House seemed to labor under the impression that GO DOWN, MOSES should be titled 'and other stories.' I remember the shock (mild) I got when I saw the printed title page. I say, reprint it, call it simply GO DOWN, MOSES, which was the way I sent it to you 8 years ago" (*SLWF*, pp. 284–85).

11 February   Faulkner writes to Cowley, who is trying to persuade Faulkner to accept the idea of a feature article on him in *Life*, where such an article had just appeared on Hemingway: "I will protest to the last: no photographs, no recorded documents."[132]

Spring   Director Clarence Brown films *Intruder in the Dust* in

---

[132] *TFCF*, p. 126; *SLWF*, p. 285.

Oxford, and Faulkner is very reluctant to collaborate. According to Joseph Blotner, however, he did rework the final scene of the script. This is unknown to Warner Bros. because of the contract which still binds Faulkner (*FAB,* p. 1278).

Summer   Joan Williams, a young student and the author of a prize-winning short story, visits Faulkner at Rowan Oak.

11 October   World premiere of *Intruder in the Dust* at the Lyric Theatre in Oxford. Faulkner attends at the insistence of his Aunt Alabama (McLean).

14 October   Faulkner gives permission to Virgil Thompson to make an opera of *The Wild Palms,* a project later abandoned by the composer.

27 November   Publication of *Knight's Gambit.*[133] In Stockholm, fifteen out of the eighteen members of the Swedish Academy vote to award Faulkner the Nobel Prize for literature. Since a unanimous vote is required, the awarding of the prize is delayed by a year.

1950   *2–12 February*   In New York, Faulkner sees both Ruth Ford and Joan Williams again.

13 February   From Rowan Oak, Faulkner sends Joan Williams three pages of notes outlining the plot of *Requiem for a Nun.*[134]

22 February   In a letter to Joan Williams in which he says that he has written a dozen pages (an outline of act 1 of the future play), he refers to the "rumors" about the Nobel Prize: "I had rather be in the same pigeon hole with Dreiser and Sher-

---

[133] The volume contains: "Smoke" (from *Doctor Martino*); "Monk" (*Scribner's,* May 1937, pp. 16–24); "Hand Upon the Waters" (*The Saturday Evening Post,* 4 November 1939, pp. 14ff.); "Tomorrow" (*The Saturday Evening Post,* 23 November 1940, pp. 22ff.); "An Error in Chemistry" (*Ellery Queen's Mystery Magazine,* June 1946, pp. 4–19); and "Knight's Gambit," which was published here for the first time.

[134] This title had already been mentioned by the writer in a letter to Harrison Smith dated October 1933. See also *17 December 1933*. According to Joseph Blotner (*FAB,* pp. 1309 ff.), it seems that Faulkner was actually offering Joan Williams a canvas on which she could paint. His letter of 13 February begins with these words: "You can begin work here." A student of Bard College, Joan Williams had just published a short story in *Mademoiselle* (August 1949). Later, she would publish a novel, *The Morning and the Evening* (1961), that was clearly influenced by *The Sound and the Fury* and *As I Lay Dying.*

wood Anderson, than with Sinclair Lewis and Mrs. Chinahand Buck" (*SLWF*, p. 299).[135]

26 March Faulkner's first public letter published outside Oxford appears in the Memphis *Commercial Appeal* on the subject of the sentencing by a Mississippi court of Leon Turner, the killer of three black children, to a simple prison sentence (*ESPL*, pp. 203–04).

9 April Faulkner writes a second letter on the same subject, in reply to a reader's reply to the first (*ESPL*, p. 205).

May Faulkner sends Joan Williams scenes 1 and 2 of act 2 of *Requiem for a Nun*. However, on 15 May he writes to Robert Haas: "I realise more than ever that I cant write a play, this may have to be rewritten by someone who can. It may be a novel as it is" (*SLWF*, pp. 302–03).

19 May Faulkner writes to Joan Williams: "Am about done with my version of 3 act. It is not a play, will have to be rewritten as a play. It is now some kind of novel" (*SLWF*, p. 304).

22 May Faulkner writes to Haas: "I have finished first draft of the play. I will rewrite it. That is, my version or complete job will be a story told in seven play-scenes, inside a novel" (*SLWF*, p. 305).

12 June Faulkner writes to the secretary of the American Academy of Arts and Letters to thank him for the Howells Medal for distinguished work in American fiction, which has just been awarded to him: "A man works for a fairly simple—limited—range of things: money, women, glory; all nice to have, but glory's best, and the best of glory is from his peers . . ." (*ESPL*, p. 206).

1 July Faulkner sends to Harold Ober a "by-product" of his play, a typescript of twenty-four pages entitled "A Name for the City," which will serve as the first of the three narrative prologues of *Requiem for a Nun* (*SLWF*, p. 306).

21 August Publication of the *Collected Stories,* the third and last collection of stories published by Faulkner. It includes

---

[135] Neither the first nor the second received the Nobel Prize for literature; the third received it in 1930, and the fourth in 1938.

forty-two of the forty-six stories published in magazines since 1930 and excludes those which had been incorporated into the volumes entitled *The Unvanquished, The Hamlet, Go Down, Moses* and *Knight's Gambit*. [136]

1 September   With a fine touch of humor, Faulkner takes a

---

[136] The table of contents of the *Collected Stories* is particularly interesting as it was conceived by Faulkner himself, including the "section-designations" (*TFCF*, pp. 116–17; *SLWF*, pp. 276–77):*

  I. THE COUNTRY
    Barn Burning (1939)
    Shingles for the Lord (1943)
    The Tall Men (1941)
    A Bear Hunt (1934)
    Two Soldiers (1942)**
  II. THE VILLAGE
    A Rose for Emily (1930; reprinted in *T13*)
    Hair (1931; reprinted in *T13*)
    Centaur in Brass (1932)
    Dry September (1931; reprinted in *T13*)
    Death Drag (1932; reprinted in *DrM*)
    Elly (1934; reprinted in *DrM*)
    Uncle Willy (1935)
    Mule in the Yard (1934)
    That Will Be Fine (1935)
    That Evening Sun (1931; reprinted in *T13*)
  III. THE WILDERNESS
    Red Leaves (1930; reprinted in *T13*)
    A Justice (1931)
    A Courtship (1948)
    Lo! (1934)
  IV. THE WASTELAND
    Ad Astra (1931; reprinted in *T13*)
    Victory (first published in *T13*)
    Crevasse (first published in *T13*)
    Turnabout (1932; reprinted in *DrM*)
    All the Dead Pilots (first published in *T13*)
  V. THE MIDDLE GROUND
    Wash (1934; reprinted in *DrM*)
    Honor (1930; reprinted in *DrM*)
    Dr Martino (1931; reprinted in *DrM*)
    Fox Hunt (1931; reprinted in *DrM*)***
    My Grandmother Millard (1943)
    Golden Land (1935)
    There Was a Queen (1933; reprinted in *DrM*)
    A Mountain Victory (1932; reprinted in *DrM*)

stand against the prohibition of beer in Lafayette County, where whiskey is freely available on the black market, by circulating 1,500 copies of a protest known as the "Beer Broadside" ("To the Voters of Oxford," *ESPL*, pp. 207–08).

5 September   Publication of the Modern Library edition of *Light in August*.

10 November   The Swedish Academy chooses William Faulkner and Bertrand Russell as corecipients of the Nobel Prize for literature. Faulkner first refuses to go to Stockholm; then pressed by the State Department, the Swedish Ambassador to the United States, and his own family, he agrees. "After all," he is supposed to have said, pretending he was only agreeing to go in order to give his daughter a chance to travel, "every young girl ought to see Paris" (*FAB*, p. 1369).

11 November   Commenting on the award, the *New York Times* writes: "Incest and rape are perhaps widespread distractions in the Jefferson, Mississippi of Faulkner, but not elsewhere in the United States." The *New York Herald* was hardly more enthusiastic: "Nothing would justify an open quarrel with regard to the Prize, even though one would have preferred the choice of a laureate more smiling in a world which is gradually getting darker."

16 November   Faulkner leaves Oxford for his annual hunting trip in the Mississippi Delta.

3 December   In Princeton, Maurice Edgar Coindreau,

VI. BEYOND

Beyond (1933; reprinted in *DrM*)
Black Music (first published in *DrM*)
The Leg (first published in *DrM*)
Mistral (first published in *T13*)
Divorce in Naples (first published in *T13*)
Carcassonne (first published in *T13*)

In his letter to Cowley of 1 November 1948, Faulkner added to this outline the following sentence: "I will write a foreword for it." As far is known, he never did.

*After each title, I am putting in parentheses the date of the first publication (in a magazine or in one of the two previous collections, *These Thirteen* [1931] and *Doctor Martino* [1934]), followed by the abbreviated title of the collection in which the story had already been reprinted—if at all.

**"Shall not Perish" (first published in 1943) was added here.

***"Pennsylvania Station" (first published in 1934), "Artist at Home" (first published in 1933), and "The Brooch" (first published in 1936) were added here.

shocked by the comments of the national press concerning Faulkner's Nobel Prize, writes in *France-Amérique,* in which he has published an article entitled "William Faulkner: The Nobel Prize in Literature" the week before: "I admit that one of the reasons which determined me to write today about the author of *Sanctuary* is the extreme reserve—not to put it more strongly—with which the American press seems to have received the news that William Faulkner had been awarded the Nobel Prize" (*TTWF,* p. 67).

7 December   Faulkner is in New York with his daughter Jill. He dines with his publishers and with Coindreau.

8 December   Faulkner and Jill fly to Stockholm.

10 December   Faulkner delivers his acceptance speech (*ESPL,* pp. 119–21) before the Swedish Academy. During the ceremony, he makes the acquaintance of Else Jonsson, the widow of Thorsten Jonsson.[137]

12 December   Faulkner and Jill land at Le Bourget airport in Paris.

15 December   They leave France for London, then on to Shannon, New York, and Memphis. They reach Oxford on 18 December.

In 1955, Faulkner would write: "Suddenly about five years ago and with no warning to myself, I adopted the habit of travel. Since then I have seen (a little of some, a little more of others) the Far and Middle East, North Africa, Europe and Scandinavia" (*ESPL,* p. 101). Joseph Blotner has calculated that, aside from his first two trips to Europe in 1925 and in 1950, Faulkner left his country six times between 1951 and 1961 and spent a total of eight months abroad. These trips, undertaken as official missions, were for the most part at the request of the Cultural Services of the State Department. The good will which Faulkner showed in accepting them must be interpreted as the reaction of a man who had a strong sense of duty.

Nevertheless, Faulkner often gave the impression of being

---

[137] See *May 1946* and note *130.*

freer during the course of these years than ever before (apart from his very first trip, of course), especially if one thinks of the many difficulties he experienced during the 1930s and of the demands made on him during the 1940s. It was as though world recognition accompanied the end of a long and tense interior exile. And if this freedom, new to him and late to come, did not necessarily mean happiness, at least pleasures were not absent from it.

1951   *1 January*   Faulkner writes to Robert Haas: "Now, I want to finish the Requiem for a Nun mss. so I wont divert to the other one [*A Fable*] until this is done" (*SLWF,* p. 311).

February   Publication of *Notes on a Horsethief* by the Levee Press, Greenville, Mississippi, in an edition limited to 975 copies, all signed by the author. The 71-page text that would, after revision, be incorporated into *A Fable,* is described by Hodding Carter, coowner of the press with Ben Wasson, as "a dangling participle" from a work-in-progress.

1 February–4 March   At Howard Hawks's request, Faulkner is in Hollywood to rework a script entitled "The Left Hand of God" for Twentieth Century-Fox. He is paid $2,000 a week. This was the last and best paid of his Hollywood stints. He even earned a bonus by finishing the script in four weeks. Faulkner suggests to Joan Williams that she accompany him to Hollywood. But in Hollywood he and Meta Carpenter become lovers again.

March   Saxe Commins accepts, on Faulkner's behalf, the National Book Award for *Collected Stories.*

2 April   Commins receives the prologue and act 2 of *Requiem for a Nun* along with a note asking him to check the accuracy of the quotation "In the beginning was the Word / Superfetation of Tò Én," taken from T. S. Eliot's poem "Mr. Eliot's Sunday Morning Service," which Faulkner wants to use following the title, "The Golden Dome."

15–29 April   After a brief stop in London with his publishers Chatto & Windus, Faulkner lands at Le Bourget airport in Paris. Entertained by the Gallimards and in particular by Monique Salomon, a friend of Else Jonsson who joins them from Sweden, Faulkner visits Verdun, which he wanted to see for his work on the conclusion to *A Fable*: "I have one more to do, the big one (Verdun) and then I have a feeling that I shall be through, can break the pencil and cast it all away, that I have spent 30 years anguishing and sweating over, never to trouble me again," he wrote Else Jonsson on 23 May (*SLWF*, p. 314).

25 May French President Vincent Auriol bestows the award of Legion of Honor upon Faulkner.

28 May Faulkner addresses Jill's graduating class at University High School in Oxford (*ESPL*, pp. 122–24).

Mid-June Just as *Requiem for a Nun* is finished and sent for typesetting, Faulkner is told by Ruth Ford that Lemuel Ayers, a young producer, is interested in it. Greatly tempted by the prospect of a stage production of his work, Faulkner replies: "the play, part, was written for you, so no contract is needed." He adds: "I have already thought of how to get the husband into the second act, and so break up the long speeches" (*SLWF*, p. 318).

July Faulkner is in New York to adapt *Requiem for a Nun* into a play with Ruth Ford and Lemuel Ayers.

13 August Back in Oxford, Faulkner cables Harrison Smith to ask that he stop a reporter from *Life* (Robert Coughlan) from coming to interview him.

19 September Faulkner and his wife are in Wellesley, Massachusetts, as Jill enrolls at Pine Manor Junior College.

25 September Faulkner turns over the responsibility of rights to the "play REQUIEM FOR A NUN" to Harold Ober (*SLWF*, p. 322).

27 September Publication of *Requiem for a Nun,* which James B. Meriwether describes as "a novel in the form of a three-act play with a narrative prologue to each act" (*LCWF*, p. 36).

2–17 October Faulkner is in Cambridge, Massachusetts, to work on the adaptation of *Requiem for a Nun* with Lemuel Ayers, Ruth Ford, and Albert Marre, the director of the Brattle Theatre.

25 October The *Oxford Eagle* announces that the premiere of the play will be in Cambridge on 10 November, "for a trial run of two weeks before the first presentation in New York at the beginning of January."

26 October   Faulkner is in New Orleans to receive the award of the Legion of Honor from the French Consul.

5 November   Faulkner is once again in Cambridge to work with Albert Marre.

17–23 November   Faulkner, back in Oxford, gathers with his friends for their annual hunt.

1952 *January*   Albert Marre comes to Oxford to discuss the problem of financing the play, particularly in view of the planned spring production in Paris. Following this discussion Faulkner writes a long letter to Saxe Commins (*SLWF*, pp. 325–26).

Mid-March   Faulkner is invited to the Festival "Oeuvres du XXe Siècle" organized by the French Congress for the Liberty of Culture. He does not yet know whether the play will be performed, as planned, at the Théâtre des Champs-Elysées on 30 May.

6 April   Faulkner accompanies Shelby Foote to Corinth, Mississippi, for the ninetieth anniversary of the Battle of Shiloh. [138]

9 April   Faulkner writes to Else Jonsson that the play will not be performed in Paris because of financial reasons—the $15,000 needed above and beyond the $7,000 that the organizers of the festival had offered could not be raised. "In spite of the uncertainty about the play, he, at least, would be going to Paris. The French government's plans for the *Oeuvres du XXe Siècle* festival were quite firm. Not only would there be ballets, concerts, and cultural exhibits, there would also be a writers' conference. They had offered to pay all his expenses, and he had told Joan [Williams] that with his 'Legion d'honneur and the Nobel and all the other hurrah,' he did not feel that he could decline the invitation." [139]

---

[138] In the same year, 1952, Shelby Foote published his best-known novel, *Shiloh* (Dial Press). See also note 112.

[139] Joseph Blotner, *Faulkner: A Biography,* one-volume edition, revised, updated, condensed (New York: Random House, 1984), p. 552.

15 May Faulkner speaks to about 5,000 members and guests of the Delta Council in Cleveland, Mississippi (*ESPL,* pp. 126–34).

19 May Faulkner is in Paris and met at Le Bourget airport by Monique and Jean-Jacques Salomon. On 19 April he had written to Else Jonsson: "I will not be too involved in Paris. I decline to be a delegate to anything; the words 'delegate' and 'freedom' in the same sentence are, to me, not only incongruous but terrifying too. I will not accept any commitment. I will pay my own way, give that time to the festival which will meet my conscience. That is, I will be a free agent in Paris, as far as I believe now. I will attend what meetings I wish, will leave when I want to" (*SLWF,* pp. 330–31).

30 May At the Salle Gaveau in Paris, after being introduced by Denis de Rougemont and in the presence of André Malraux, Faulkner says a few words and receives an ovation. The text of his brief speech is published in *Arts* No. 362 (5–11 June), p. 6.

31 May After a stay in the Clinique Rémy de Gourmont for treatment of back pain caused by an old injury and for the problems with alcohol that the pain led to, Faulkner leaves France for London, where he is the guest of Harold Raymond of Chatto & Windus.

4–14 June Faulkner rests in Oslo in the company of Else Jonsson.

17 June At home again, Faulkner resumes his relationship with Joan Williams. He continues his work on *A Fable,* with more and more difficulty.[140]

12–26 September Suffering again from acute back pain, Faulkner is hospitalized in Memphis.

8–21 October Faulkner is hospitalized again after a fall on the stairway of Rowan Oak. Refusing obstinately to undergo surgery, he is told he must wear a steel brace.

November A television team financed by the Ford Founda-

---

[140] It is a fact as uncharacteristic as it is well-known that he drew a synopsis of the novel on the walls of his "office" at Rowan Oak; see the facsimile in *FAB,* p. 1464; for a complete transcription, see James Webb, "Faulkner Writes *A Fable,*" *University of Mississippi Studies in English,* 7 (1966), 7–10.

tion comes to Oxford to make a short documentary film on Faulkner.

30 November   Faulkner is in Princeton staying with Saxe and Dorothy Commins and working on *A Fable* when he is interviewed by a young Frenchman, Loïc Bouvard. Their conversation deals with God ("If you don't reckon with God you won't wind up anywhere"); time ("man is never time's slave"); man ("man is free, and he is responsible, terribly responsible"); France; her writers ("I feel very close to Proust") and philosophers ("I agree pretty much with Bergson's theory of the fluidity of time");[141] and the future ("Sometimes I think of doing what Rimbaud did—yet, I will certainly keep on writing as long as I live.")[142]

December   After a recurrence of his back pain and subsequent stay in a hospital where he is given electric shock treatment, Faulkner spends the end of the year partly in Princeton and partly in New York, where, in Commins's office at Random House, he continues to work on *A Fable*. As is his custom, however, he is back in Oxford for Christmas.

1953   *31 January*   After arranging to be away from Oxford for a much longer absence than usual, Faulkner arrives in New York. He stays first with Harrison Smith, where his back pain and alcoholism, the one invariably provoking the other, force him again to be hospitalized. He then visits Robert Haas and finally goes to his favorite hotel, the Algonquin. He works on *A Fable* as much as he can. In addition, he adapts the story, "The Brooch," for television. Also, he is "thinking about writing [his] memoirs. That is, it will be a book in the shape of a biography but actually about half fiction . . ."[143]

---

[141] I am convinced that these statements concerning Proust and Bergson a) came too late to suggest a real influence, and b) can at least partially be explained by the fact that they were prompted by a Frenchman's questions.

[142] See *LITG*, pp. 68–73. The original French version of this interview was published in *Bulletin de l'Association amicale universitaire France-Amérique*, (January (1954), pp. 23–29.

[143] This description announces the essay, "Mississippi," which was published in *Holiday* (April 1954) (*ESPL*, pp. 11–43).

March   Faulkner is again hospitalized and undergoes a variety of tests, the results of all of which are normal. Faulkner's friends in New York then prevail upon him to consult a neurologist and a psychiatrist. Faulkner refuses to discuss his mother with the latter.

18 April   Faulkner is called back to Rowan Oak after his wife suffers a hemorrhage followed by a heart attack.

29 April   In a letter to Joan Williams, Faulkner expresses fear that he will soon be "getting toward the end, the bottom of the barrel" as a writer (*SLWF*, p. 380).

9 May   Once again in New York, at the Haases, Faulkner meets e. e. cummings and Dylan Thomas.

8 June   Faulkner addresses Jill's graduating class at Pine Manor Junior College (*ESPL*, pp. 135–42). *Atlantic* publishes "A Note on Sherwood Anderson" (*ESPL*, pp. 3–10).[144]

August   While Random House is preparing *The Faulkner Reader*, Faulkner, alone at Rowan Oak, finishes the "scene of the three temptations" for *A Fable*.

8 September   Faulkner is hospitalized in Memphis.

28 September, 5 October   *Life* publishes an article in two parts on Faulkner by Robert Coughlan, a publication Faulkner had tried hard to prevent.[145]

October 7   Faulkner writes to Phil Mullen, associate editor of the *Oxford Eagle*, who had helped Robert Coughlan gather material but who now writes to tell Faulkner that he had not supplied the personal details about the family: "What a commentary. Sweden gave me the Nobel Prize. France gave me the Legion d'Honneur. All my native land did for me was to invade my privacy over my protest and my plea. No wonder people in the rest of the world dont like us, since we seem to have neither taste nor courtesy, and know and believe in nothing but money and it doesn't much matter how you get it" (*SLWF*, p. 354).

November   The foreword to *The Faulkner Reader* (see *1 April 1954*) is dated "New York, November 1953." The last page of

---

[144] See *26 April 1925* for Faulkner's first homage to Anderson.

[145] See *11 February 1949* and *13 August 1951*. Robert Coughlan also published a book entitled *The Private World of William Faulkner* (New York: Harper and Brothers, 1954; repr. New York: Cooper Square, 1972).

the manuscript of *A Fable,* numbered 654, says "Oxford, December, 1944 / New York and Princeton, November 1953." The liaison with Joan Williams comes to an end, though Faulkner continues to write to her.

16 November   Albert Camus' agent writes for permission to adapt *Requiem for a Nun* for the stage. Faulkner is agreeable, but he wishes that Ruth Ford be consulted first.

1 December   At Howard Hawks's request, Faulkner arrives in Geneva on his way to Egypt, where he will assist Hawks in filming *Land of the Pharaohs* (their last collaboration). They go to Stresa to work together.

25 December   In St. Moritz, Faulkner meets Jean Stein, a young American woman staying in Switzerland.

26 December   Faulkner is in Stockholm with Else Jonsson.

1954   *1 January*   Faulkner is in England with Harold Raymond.

6 January   He is back in St. Moritz with Jean Stein.

Mid-January   Faulkner spends a few days in Paris with Jean Stein and Monique Salomon, whose daughter is his goddaughter.

19 January   He joins Howard Hawks, Humphrey Bogart, and Lauren Bacall in Rome.

4 February   From Rome, Faulkner writes to Saxe Commins inquiring about the possible rights William Bacher and Henry Hathaway might have for providing material used in his creation of *A Fable.*

15 February   After a weekend in Paris, Faulkner, in very poor physical condition, joins Howard Hawks in Cairo.

6 March   Joan Williams marries Ezra Bowen.

22 March   Jill Faulkner writes to her father that she has met Paul D. Summers, a young lieutenant at West Point, whom she wishes to marry. She asks her father to return home.

29 March   Faulkner frees himself from the contract with Howard Hawks and Harry Kurnitz. He flies to Paris where he is met by Monique Salomon, Else Jonsson, and Jean Stein. He makes the last corrections on *A Fable.*

1 April   Publication of *The Faulkner Reader.* [146]

---

[146] This anthology, which was chosen by the Book-of-the-Month Club, is very

April *Holiday* publishes "Mississippi" (*ESPL,* pp. 11–43), one of Faulkner's finest nonfiction pieces. This chronicle combines three components: history, his childhood, and his own work, all set against the background of his native state. It is probably in April that he writes a short "blurb" for *A Fable* (which is not published until 1973).[147] It begins: "This is not a pacifist book. On the contrary, this writer holds almost as short a brief for pacifism as for war itself, for the reason that pacifism does not work, cannot cope with the forces which produce wars" (*AFM,* pp. 162–63). Saxe Commins seems to have been the one who decides against using it.

5–6 April Faulkner is in the American Hospital in Paris.

12 April From Paris, Faulkner has Monique Salomon cable Saxe Commins: "FORGOT JUDAS MISERY DESIRE REWRITE ONE SECTION PLAN ARRIVE 20 APRIL OR WILL CABLE TO SEND SECTION HERE" (*FAB,* p. 1493; *SLWF,* p. 363).

19 April After revisiting Verdun, in the company of Monique Salomon and her husband, Faulkner leaves Paris for New York.

End of April Faulkner is back in Oxford after an absence of six months. Rather uncharacteristically, Faulkner reads whole sections of *A Fable* to his wife and daughter, to whom the book is dedicated.

End of June Faulkner accepts an invitation from the State Department to attend an international writers conference in São Paulo in August.

2 August Publication of *A Fable* which, Malcolm Cowley writes, "is likely to stand above other novels of the year like a cathedral, if an imperfect and unfinished one."[148]

---

different from *The Portable Faulkner;* it contains one complete novel, *The Sound and the Fury,* and three long short stories, or "novellas," as they are called on the book jacket. These "novellas" were published in 1958 with the title *Three Famous Short Novels:* "The Bear" (from *Go Down, Moses,* including chapter 4); "Old Man" (from *The Wild Palms*); and "Spotted Horses" (from *The Hamlet*); as well as eight stories from the *Collected Stories,* some selections from *The Unvanquished, Light in August,* and *Requiem for a Nun;* and the text of the Nobel Prize acceptance speech. Faulkner wrote the foreword to this volume.

[147] This statement first appeared in the *Mississippi Quarterly,* 26 (Summer 1973), 416–17; then in *AFM,* pp. 162–63.

[148] *New York Herald Tribune,* 1 August 1954.

7 August Faulkner arrives in Lima.

11 August Faulkner is interviewed in São Paulo.

16 August Faulkner returns to Oxford.

21 August Jill Faulkner and Paul D. Summers, Jr., are married. The latter will subsequently leave the army and become a lawyer.

30 September In New York since 10 September, Faulkner records some excerpts from his work for Caedmon and revises the story "Race at Morning," which Ober sells for $2,500, a record price, to *The Saturday Evening Post.*

18 October Back in Oxford, Faulkner reads the manuscript of Robert Coughlan's book *The Private World of William Faulkner* (Harper and Brothers, 1954) (see *28 September–5 October 1953*). Outraged, he writes an essay first entitled "Freedom of the Press," then "On Privacy (The American Dream: What Happened to It?)" (*ESPL,* pp. 62–75; see *14 April 1955*).

25 December Faulkner spends Christmas at the home of Saxe and Dorothy Commins in the company of Jean Stein.

One short story was published in 1954:

"Sepulture South: Gaslight," *Harper's Bazaar,* 88 (December) pp. 85ff.; reprinted in *USWF.*

1955 Faulkner is now a public figure. He no longer refuses to appear in public in his own country, and, even though he may hesitate at times, he usually accepts the requests of the State Department to participate in cultural events abroad. In 1955 he takes a trip of nearly three months to seven different countries, and he takes a definite position as a moderate, if not liberal, southerner in the increasingly heated debate over school integration. Though he is no longer "driven" by the "demon" of writing nor tortured by the need for money, he nonetheless keeps on writing. Since the long and strenuous effort of *A Fable,* however, it is clear that he is no longer the man of twenty-five years of inner exile and that his literary creation is no longer as intense, or "hot" (his favorite metaphor when speaking of getting ready to write) as it used to be.

21 January Faulkner signs a contract for a volume of hunting stories to be called *Big Woods* (see *14 October*).

25 January   Faulkner speaks in New York on receiving the National Book Award for Fiction (for *A Fable*; *ESPL*, pp. 143–45).

30 January   Publication in the *New York Times Book Review* of an interview by Harvey Breit in which Faulkner repeats his opinion of Hemingway: "He stayed within what he knew. He did it fine, but he didn't try for the impossible"—a judgment that does not seem to include *The Old Man and the Sea*, about which he had written three years earlier that it was "his best book" (*ESPL*, p. 193).

End of February   In New York, Faulkner signs the final agreement giving Albert Camus permission to adapt *Requiem for a Nun*.

11 March   *Go Down, Moses* is published in the Modern Library edition.

20 March   Publication of the first of a series of four letters to the Memphis *Commercial Appeal* on the subject of school segregation. Faulkner's argument is that the Mississippi schools are already so bad for whites that it is absurd to expect that racial integration will make them better. But it is even more absurd "to raise additional taxes to establish another system at best only equal to that one which is already not good enough" (*ESPL*, pp. 215–16). The three other letters were published on 3, 10, and 17 April. They earned him much hostility in his native state, including that of his own brother, John.

14 April   First at the University of Oregon, then at the University of Montana, on 17 April, Faulkner delivers a speech entitled "Freedom American Style" which is published in *Harper's* in July under the title, "On Privacy (The American Dream: What Happened to It?)." According to James B. Meriwether, Faulkner "had planned a book of five or six related essays, to be called *The American Dream*. He wrote, however, only two chapters of it, 'On Privacy' and 'On Fear,' in 1955 and 1956" (*ESPL*, p. vii).

7 May   Faulkner reports on the eighty-first Kentucky Derby for *Sports Illustrated* (see *ESPL*, pp. 52–61).

16 May   Back in Oxford, Faulkner agrees to go to Japan in August to participate in a "seminar," provided that he be allowed to return by way of Europe, even if it is at his own expense. However, as he writes on 5 July: "If there is anything I can do after Japan, between there and America, which can help toward a better understanding of our country and our State Dept., I dont need to say that I want to do it, and will hold myself available" (*SLWF,* p. 383). On 8 July, he nonetheless insists that he is not a man of letters and that he will speak simply as an individual "who is interested in and believes in people, humanity, and has some concern about man's condition and his future, if he is not careful" (*SLWF,* p. 384).

12 June From Oxford, where the quarrel over school and university integration is now raging, Faulkner writes to Else Jonsson: "I am doing what I can. I can see the possible time when I shall have to leave my native state, something as the Jew had to flee from Germany during Hitler. I hope that wont happen of course. But at times I think that nothing but a disaster, a military defeat even perhaps, will wake America up and enable us to save ourselves, or what is left. This is a depressing letter, I know. But human beings are terrible. One must believe well in man to endure him, wait out his folly and savagery and inhumanity" (*SLWF,* p. 382).

2 July *Land of the Pharaohs,* Faulkner's last work for Warner Bros., is released.

1 August Faulkner arrives in Tokyo. Joseph Blotner writes: "No period of Faulkner's life is better known than the three weeks which he spent in Japan. He was interviewed ceaselessly and his activities were reported in detail."[149]

5 August Faulkner leaves Tokyo for Nagano, where he takes part in a seminar whose proceedings, along with two speeches entitled "Impressions of Japan" and "To the Youth of Japan," are published, first in Tokyo,[150] then in *LITG* (pp. 84–198).

16 August Faulkner leaves Nagano for Tokyo.

23 August Faulkner leaves Japan for Manila, where he

---

[149] Joseph Blotner, "William Faulkner, Roving Ambassador," *International Educational and Cultural Exchange* (United States Advisory Commission on International Educational and Cultural Affairs), Summer 1966, p. 7.

[150] Robert A. Jelliffe, ed., *Faulkner at Nagano* (Tokyo: Kenkyusha Ltd., 1956).

spends three days with his stepdaughter, Victoria, her daughter, Victoria Hamilton, and her second husband, William Fielden. He is also interviewed and delivers his speech on the American Dream at the university. The Manila interviews were published separately in 1956; they are reprinted in *LITG* (pp. 199–214).

28 August   Faulkner arrives in Italy, where he stays until 16 September with friends, including Jean Stein. He takes part in seminars in Rome, Naples, and Milan, where he is received by his Italian publisher, Arnoldo Mondadori. According to an Italian newspaper, Faulkner's presence is "the cultural event in Italy this summer."

6 September   From Rome, Faulkner issues a dispatch on the murder of Emmett Till, a young Negro from Chicago who has been killed while in Mississippi. "Because if we in America have reached that point in our desperate culture when we must murder children, no matter for what reason or what color, we don't deserve to survive, and probably won't" (*ESPL*, p. 223).

16 September   Faulkner leaves Italy for Munich, where *Requiem for a Nun* is playing (*FAB*, p. 1574).

17 September   Faulkner leaves Munich for Paris, where he spends two weeks.

19 September   Faulkner holds a press conference at the American Embassy.

26 September   He records about fifteen pages of *A Fable* for the United States Information Service.

29 September   Faulkner attends a garden party at Gallimard. Several interviews are published, one of which by Madeleine Chapsal, "Lion in the Garden," gives its title to the collection of interviews published in 1968 by James B. Meriwether and Michael Millgate.

7 October   Faulkner leaves Paris for London.

12–17 October   Faulkner is in Reykjavik, Iceland, where the ritual program of conferences and interviews takes place once more. Faulkner justifies the presence of American troops in Iceland in the name of liberty.

14 October   Publication of *Big Woods*, illustrated (as *The Unvanquished* was) by Edward Shenton. It is "a collection of four previously published hunting stories. Five brief narrative pieces are used, at the beginning and end of the book, and between each story, to set or change the mood; Faulkner has described them, in an interview in the *New York Times Book Review,* January 30, 1955, as 'interrupted catalysts' " (*LCWF,* p. 39).[151] The book is dedicated "To Saxe Commins. From the author / to the editor: we have never seen eye to eye / but we have always looked / toward the same thing."

10 November In Memphis, along with Benjamin Mays and Cecil Sims,[152] Faulkner addresses the Southern Historical Association in the Peabody Hotel, where much effort is needed for blacks to be admitted. This explains the title under which the text of Faulkner's speech is published in the Memphis *Commercial Appeal*: "A mixed audience hears Faulkner condemn the 'shame' of segregation."[153]

20 November Under the title "A reader from Mississippi writes that the author is turning his back on the southern tradition," the Memphis *Commercial Appeal* publishes a letter by Edwin White of Lexington, Mississippi, protesting Faulkner's recent speech. White's argument in favor of segregation is: "White parents in the South will not accept causing the death of their race by sending their children to integrated schools."

Thirty years later, it is difficult to imagine the situation in which Faulkner had put himself after he had taken publicly and definitely, although not without qualms,[154] a firm stand against segregation. Hodding Carter, a liberal from Greenville, Mis-

---

[151] These were materials drawn from *Requiem for A Nun,* from "Red Leaves" and "A Justice," from "Mississippi" and "Delta Autumn" *(Go Down, Moses).* See *LIG,* p. 83.

[152] Mays was the president of Atlanta's Morehouse College, and Sims was a lawyer from Nashville.

[153] The text in *ESPL,* pp. 146–51, was printed from the revised and expanded version first published in *Three Views of the Segregation Decision* (Atlanta, Southern Regional Council, 1956).

[154] For example, Faulkner did regret that the decision of 17 May 1954, putting an end to segregation in the schools, had to be accomplished by the federal government.

sissippi, who had long known Faulkner, wrote in 1957 that the writer "had ventured beyond the ultimate Southern pale; and nothing, not even the initial reaction to *Sanctuary*, could match what happened to him since."[155] There is no doubt that he was subjected to pressures that went as far as threats from anonymous telephone callers during the night[156] and that he was rejected by his own brother, John. His reasonable, moderate stand was not understood any better by the liberals from the North, both white and black.[157] As far as his literary career is concerned, the least one can say is that these circumstances did not help Faulkner's creativity.

2 December   Faulkner writes to Jean Stein: "I have just started on another novel, the second Snopes volume" (*FAB*, p. 1556).

8 December   Faulkner writes a letter concerning the race question on the verso of page forty of the typescript of *The Town*.

Two stories were published in 1955:
   1. "Race at Morning," *The Saturday Evening Post*, 227 (5 March) pp. 26ff.; revised for *Big Woods;* reprinted in *USWF*.
   2. "By the People," *Mademoiselle*, 41 (October) pp. 86ff.; incorporated in *The Mansion* (1959).

1956 *February*   At the University of Alabama tension is mounting over the admission of a black student, Autherine Lucy. In New York, Faulkner seeks to make the voice of a concerned southerner heard in the North. He asks Harold Ober to sell "On Fear: the South in Labor" (*ESPL*, pp. 92–106), preferably to *Harper's*,[158] and to find him a channel for a public statement.

---

[155] "Faulkner and His Folk," *Princeton University Library Chronicle*, 18 (Spring 1957), 95–107.

[156] See his letter to Jean Stein dated *28 or 29 October 1955* (*SLWF*, p. 388).

[157] In this respect it is particularly interesting to compare Faulkner's views with those of Ralph Ellison, born in Oklahoma, in *Shadow and Act*, and James Baldwin, a New Yorker, in *Nobody Knows My Name*.

[158] Faulkner did so because *Harper's* had already published "On Privacy" in July 1955: see *14 April 1955*. *Harper's* finally published "On Fear" in June 1956.

Both attempts fail, but, on 21 February, in Commins's office, Faulkner grants an unfortunate interview to Russell W. Howe, a correspondent of the London *Sunday Times* in New York, with whom he gets along poorly. The reporter has Faulkner saying that he would "fight for Mississippi against the United States, even if it meant going out into the street and shooting Negroes." It is absurd, and Faulkner tries to correct the unfortunate statement in three successive letters addressed to national magazines that have repeated his initial declaration. But harm has been done and cannot be easily undone. In *The Reporter* of 19 April, Russell Howe publishes a rejoinder in which "he affirmed the accuracy of the interview, which had been 'directly transcribed,' he said, 'from verbatim shorthand notes'" (*LITG*, p. 257).

In the meantime, Faulkner grants an interview to Jean Stein which is definitely the best of all those he gave. It is published in the spring issue of *The Paris Review* and is reprinted in *Writers at Work: The Paris Review Interviews* (New York, 1958) and in *LITG*, pp. 237–56.

4 March First publication of the Howe interview in the London *Sunday Times*.

5 March *Life* publishes "A Letter to the North" in which Faulkner pleads for moderation, warning that one should not expect too much of the South (*ESPL*, pp. 86–91).

18 March ". . . the effects of the accumulated anger, fear, frustration, injury, sickness and drinking suddenly caught up with him. He began to vomit blood and collapsed into unconsciousness" (*FAB*, p. 1598). Faulkner is hospitalized at the Baptist Hospital in Memphis until 27 March.

22 March Second publication (with variants) of the Howe interview in *The Reporter*.

26 March Faulkner's grandson Paul is born in Charlottesville, Virginia, the first child of Jill and Paul D. Summers. Soon, Faulkner would agree to become writer-in-residence at the University of Virginia for a period of eight to ten weeks every year.

16 April At 88, W. E. B. Du Bois, one of the founders of the NAACP, challenges Faulkner to a debate on integration "on the steps of the courthouse of Sumner, Mississippi," the location of the trial of the murderers of Emmett Till (see 6 *September 1955*).

18 April Faulkner declines the invitation in telegram to Du Bois, which is reproduced in the *New York Times*: "I DO NOT BELIEVE THERE IS A DEBATABLE POINT BETWEEN US. WE BOTH AGREE IN ADVANCE THAT THE POSITION YOU WILL TAKE IS RIGHT MORALLY LEGALLY AND ETHICALLY. IF IT IS NOT EVIDENT TO YOU THAT THE POSITION I TAKE IN ASKING FOR MODERATION AND PATIENCE IS RIGHT PRACTICALLY THEN WE WILL BOTH WASTE OUR BREATH IN DEBATE. WILLIAM FAULKNER" (*SLWF*, p. 398).

19 April Faulkner writes a letter to *The Reporter* protesting the terms of the interview published in the London *Sunday Times* of 4 March (and reprinted by *The Reporter*): "They are statements which no sober man would make nor, it seems to me, any sane man believe" (*ESPL*, p. 225). However, Russell Howe maintains that Faulkner made the statements in question.

23 April Faulkner writes a letter to *Time* to the same effect as that to *The Reporter* (*ESPL*, p. 226).

8 May Faulkner returns to Oxford, while his wife stays in Charlottesville with their daughter.

Early June Faulkner sends to Saxe Commins what he hopes is the first third of "Snopes, Volume Two." "On Fear: the South in Labor" is finally published by *Harper's*.

27 June Faulkner sends to Harold Ober a "Letter to the Leaders in the Negro Race" which he has written in response to a request from *Ebony* after the interview in *The Reporter*, and which would appear in the September issue of the magazine (*ESPL*, pp. 107–112). Joseph Blotner comments: "He had already been called a gradualist. This essay would serve only to affirm this label in the minds of white liberals and to discredit him with Negro activists" (*FAB*, pp. 1609–10).

22 August Faulkner writes to Jean Stein, about *The Town* (probably after writing about Eula Varner's suicide): "Just finishing the book. It breaks my heart, I wrote one scene and almost cried. I thought it was just a funny book but I was wrong" (*SLWF,* p. 402).

September After the success of his "official" trips abroad, Faulkner lets himself become involved in the "People-to-People Program" of the Eisenhower administration. The aim of the program is to promote American culture behind the Iron Curtain. On 11 September, he attends a meeting in Washington at which President Eisenhower, Vice-President Richard Nixon, and Secretary of State John Foster Dulles speak. Then, with the help of Harvey Breit, an informal committee meets in New York. On 30 September, the steering committee composed of Faulkner, John Steinbeck, and Donald Hall, draws up some "resolutions" including one supporting the liberation of Ezra Pound. Three months later, Faulkner withdraws from the committee.

20 September *Requiem for a Nun,* adapted by Camus, is premiered in Paris, at the Théâtre des Mathurins. On 10 October, Faulkner cables his thanks to Mme. Harry-Baur (*SLWF,* p. 405).

Autumn In view of an exhibition of Faulkner's works to be held at the Princeton University Library in 1957, James B. Meriwether begins to compile a catalog of the available manuscripts and typescripts.[159]

8 November Date on page one of the manuscript of *The Mansion,* volume 3 of the Snopes trilogy.

10 and 16 December *Time* and the *New York Times* publish two letters written in Oxford in which Faulkner takes a stand against those who condemn the intervention of England, France, and Israel in the region of the Suez Canal (*ESPL,* pp. 227–28).

1957 *February–June* Faulkner is writer-in-residence at the University of Virginia, thanks to the Emily Clark Balch Foundation, which provides him with "a house to live in and someone to clean it." A selection of the question-and-answer periods

---

[159] See *10 May–30 August 1957.*

with the students, faculty, and faculty spouses would be published in 1959 by Professors Joseph Blotner and Frederick Gwynn under the title *Faulkner in the University*. In addition, Faulkner, like every member of the faculty, has office hours in the Department of English office at Cabell Hall. There he talks with students and professors. One of the latter, James Colvert, a former aviator, remembers the stories Faulkner would tell. Sometimes, he says, one got the impression that Faulkner "was inventing as he went along."

17 March On leave of absence from the University of Virginia, Faulkner arrives in Athens where he attends a performance of *Requiem for a Nun*. To the question, "Do you have a message for the Greek people?" he replies, "Your country is the cradle of civilized man. Your ancestors are the mothers and fathers of civilization, and of human liberty. What more do you want from me, an American farmer?" (*FAB*, pp. 1645–46).

20 March Faulkner visits Mycenae and some of the Greek islands, where he sees the light which he would refer to, two months later in Virginia, to explain the title *Light in August*.[160] About Greece he says: "[It was] the only place I was in where there was a sense of a very distant past but there was nothing inimical in it. In the other parts of the Old World there is a sense of the past but there is something Gothic and in a sense a little terrifying. . . . The people seem to function against that past that for all its remoteness in time it was still inherent in the light, the resurgence of spring, you didn't expect to see the ghost of the old Greeks, or expect to see the actual figures of the gods, but you had a sense that they were near and they were still powerful, not inimical, just powerful" (*FITU*, pp. 129–30).

28 March Faulkner receives the Silver Medal of the Athens

---

[160] See *FITU*, p. 199. See also Coindreau: "I have often thought that he must have done violence to his own feelings . . . to confirm me in my idea that *Light in August* meant *Lumière d'août*, as I had translated the phrase in 1935, and not *légère en août*, as Isabel Paterson had suggested in 1933, long before Malcolm Cowley had set forth, in a different form, the same absurd opinion" (*TTWF*, p. 100).

Academy "as one chosen by the Greek Academy to represent the principle that man shall be free" (*ESPL*, p. 152).

31 March Faulkner returns to New York.

April Back in Charlottesville, Faulkner signs a contract with producer Jerry Wald for an option on *The Hamlet*. The film, made by Martin Ritt with Orson Welles as Will Varner, would be released in 1958 under the title *The Long Hot Summer*.

1 May Publication of *The Town*. Like the first volume of the Snopes trilogy, it is dedicated to Phil Stone, "who did half of the laughing for thirty years." The last page of the novel bears the note: "Oxford-Charlottesville-Washington-New York, November 1955–September 1956."

4 May The final episode of *The Town*, entitled "The Waifs" (Faulkner's suggestion for the title is "Them Indians"), is published in *The Saturday Evening Post* (*LCWF*, p. 44). According to James B. Meriwether, "the price [$3,000] was the highest Faulkner had yet received for a contribution to a periodical."[161]

10 May–30 August Exhibition entitled "The Literary Career of William Faulkner" opens at the Princeton University Library (see *LCWF*, pp. vii–x).

22 May Faulkner speaks before the American Academy of Arts and Letters at the presentation of the Gold Medal for Fiction to John Dos Passos (*ESPL*, pp. 153–54).

26 June Faulkner leaves Charlottesville for Oxford.

15 September Another letter by Faulkner on school integration is published in the Memphis *Commercial Appeal* (*ESPL*, p. 229).

13 November Faulkner is back in Charlottesville.

December On hearing that Albert Camus has been awarded the Nobel Prize for literature, Faulkner sends him the following cable: "ON SALUT [*sic*] L'AME QUI CONSTAMMENT SE CHERCHE ET SE DEMANDE" (*FAB*, p. 1680).[162]

---

[161] James B. Meriwether, "Faulkner's Correspondence with *The Saturday Evening Post*," *The Mississippi Quarterly*, 30 (Summer 1977), 462, n. 4 (the piece was not "an episode from his novel *The Reivers*," though [see line 2]).

[162] "Hail to the soul that constantly searches and questions itself!"

1958 *January* Premiere of the film *The Tarnished Angels,* an adaptation of *Pylon* by Douglas Sirk.

29 January Faulkner begins to type chapter 3 of *The Mansion.* The president of the University of Virginia refuses to consider making Faulkner a permanent member of the faculty. According to Joseph Blotner (*FAB,* p. 1685), this was at least partly because of Faulkner's views on school segregation; indeed, this was the year when most of the schools in Albermarle County remained closed to protest integration.

February–May Faulkner's second term as writer-in-residence. In *Faulkner in the University,* only thirteen sessions are recorded (as compared to twenty-three the preceding year), but the series includes two of the most important recordings: on 20 February, "A Word to Virginians" (pp. 209–27), which contains the substance of Faulkner's views on the race issue, and on 24 April, "A Word to Young Writers" (pp. 241–48), which reflects the ideas of his Nobel Prize acceptance speech.

March Faulkner is in Princeton, then in Charlottesville, then in Oxford, and then back in Charlottesville.

8 March Faulkner is interviewed by the *New York Times* on the crisis in Little Rock, Arkansas, following Governor Faubus's decision to oppose school integration: "The reply consists in one single word: education."

31 May Back in Oxford, Faulkner declines an invitation to become part of a group of writers going to the Soviet Union: "The Russia with which I have, I hope, earned any right to spiritual kinship was the Russia which produced Dostoievsky, Tolstoy, Chekhov, Gogol, etc. That Russia is no longer there. . . . If the Russians were free, they would probably conquer the earth" (*FAB,* p. 1695).

June Faulkner types chapter 6 of *The Mansion.*

17 July Saxe Commins dies in Princeton.

18 September The Faulkners join their daughter Jill at the home of Linton Massey, a rich Virginian who collects Faulkner's works.[163]

16 November Faulkner has a brief meeting with students at

---

[163] See *1 October–23 December 1959.*

Princeton University. He begins chapter 13 of *The Mansion.*
From now on, he substitutes fox hunting in Virginia for the
annual "big hunt" in the Mississippi Delta.
2 December   Jill's second son, William, is born.

During the year 1958, Faulkner corresponds with Albert
Erskine at Random House on the changes to be made in the
Snopes trilogy that would eliminate certain inconsistencies
(particularly chronological contradictions). The endeavor,
however, soon raises complex textual problems, which Albert
Erskine and James B. Meriwether (who, after the Princeton
exhibit, has become a part-time consultant) solve differently—
as an editor and a scholar would. The situation is complicated
by the fact that Faulkner himself is not easy to deal with.
Though there seems to be no doubt that he has a growing
awareness that there should be a "unified" edition of the Snopes
trilogy (and he obviously likes the idea of seeing his three
novels in one case), he firmly resists any systematization of the
revising, or unifying, process, particularly if it means changing
what he had just written, as his letter of 7 May 1958 to Albert
Erskine shows clearly: "Premise: I am a veteran member of a
living literature. In my synonymity, 'living' equals 'motion,
change, constant alteration,' equals 'evolution,' which in my
optimistic synonymity equals 'improvement.' So if what I
write in 1958 aint better than what I wrote in 1938, I should
have stopped writing twenty years ago; or, since 'being alive'
equals 'motion,' I should be 20 years in the grave. . . . Repeat,
I would be perfectly willing to make the dud shell in MANSION
match the dud shell in HAMLET, if the MANSION version did
not offer the best dramatic moment for it" (*SLWF,* pp. 429–
30). A few days later, however, he writes to Erskine: "Have a
rewrite idea for *Mink* in *Mansion* which will match the dud
shells when he shot Houston in *Hamlet,* and will lose nothing
of *Mansion* story" (SLWF, p. 431).
Though, in many cases, there remains a doubt as to who
suggested a particular change, or even as to which changes
were made against Faulkner's intention, if not against his will,
it seems safe to say that the three original, separate editions of

The Hamlet, The Town, and *The Mansion* offer a better text than the "unified" edition of *Snopes* published in 1964. [164]

1958 saw the first (re)publication of pieces dating from Faulkner's youth when Carvel Collins made available a collection of the *New Orleans Sketches* (see *1925*).

1959   *4 January*   Faulkner is in Oxford for five weeks.
23 January   Faulkner cables his wife that he has finished *The Mansion.*
28 January   Premiere of *Requiem for a Nun* at the John Golden Theatre in New York. The U.S. is the thirteenth country in which the play is staged (see *LCWF,* 37n). Directed by Tony Richardson (the future film director), it features Ruth Ford as Temple, Zachary Scott as Gavin Stevens, and Beatrice Reading as Nancy Mannigoe. In the printed edition which appears the same year, Faulkner is careful to warn his readers: "This play was written not to be a play, but as what seemed to me the best way to tell the story in a novel. It became a play, to me, only after Ruth Ford saw it as a play and believed that only she could do it right. When in English, it is her play. When she adds to it, to make it a better play, is Ruth Ford." [165]
End of January   Faulkner is displeased to hear that Phil Stone has sold his collection of Faulkneriana to the University of Texas (*SLWF,* p. 421).
February   Faulkner settles temporarily at Farmington, near Charlottesville. He takes part in the activities of the Hunt Club; photographs, and even an oil portrait, show him proudly wearing his pink coat as a member of the club.
25 February   The *Richmond Times* announces the death, in Albermarle County, of Cornell Franklin, Estelle's first husband.

---

[164] The same problem is exemplified in the exchange of letters between Faulkner and Malcolm Cowley on the subject of the relationship between *The Sound and the Fury* and the "Compson Appendix," to be read either in *TFCF* or in *SLWF.*

[165] "When in English, it is her play" may well be a discreet allusion to the Camus adaptation, which one can prove that the Ford version borrowed from. "When she adds to it, to make it a better play" may be considered a courteous disclaimer.

9 March   Faulkner completes the final typescript of *The Mansion*. He sends "Flem," the third and last part of the novel, to Albert Erskine at Random House.

14 March . Faulkner falls from a horse at Farmington and fractures his collarbone.

26 March   The fall prevents him from being present in New York at a meeting with Albert Erskine and James B. Meriwether to work on the discrepancies in the Snopes trilogy. On 9 March he wrote to Erskine: "Do you agree that, as far as possible, this volume should be the definitive one, others can be edited in subsequent editions to conform." But, in a characteristic fashion, he added, in ink: "Unless of course the discrepancy is paradoxical and outrageous" (*SLWF*, p. 426).

June   Faulkner transfers his manuscripts and typescripts from the Princeton University Library to the Alderman Library at the University of Virginia. He goes to New York to work with Albert Erskine on the corrections of *The Mansion*.

9 June   The *New York Times* announces that Faulkner has bought a house in Charlottesville. The address is 917 Rugby Road, and he writes at least part of his last novel there.

29 June–2 July   Dates on the galleys of *The Mansion*.

1 October–23 December   An exhibition entitled "William Faulkner: 'Man Working,' 1919–1959" organized by Linton Massey opens at the Alderman Library of the University of Virginia.[166]

2 October   Faulkner speaks in Denver, Colorado, before the U.S. National Commission for U.N.E.S.C.O. (*ESPL*, pp. 166–67).

15 October   Faulkner exhibit opens at the Humanities Research Center of the University of Texas at Austin.

31 October   Harold Ober dies.

8 November   The Memphis *Commercial Appeal* publishes pho-

---

[166] See Linton R. Massey, comp., *William Faulkner: "Man Working," 1919–1962: A Catalogue of the William Faulkner Collections at the University of Virginia* (Charlottesville, University Press of Virginia, 1968), and Joan St.C. Crane and Anne E. H. Freudenberg, comp., *Man Collecting the Works of William Faulkner: An Exhibition in the University of Virginia Library Honoring Linton Reynolds Massey (1900–1974)* (Charlottesville: University Printing Office, 1975).

tographs of "The Flying Faulkners": John and his grandson; William in front of his Waco; Dean (dead since 1935); and Jimmy (John's son) in front of a jet plane.

13 November   Publication of *The Mansion,* volume 3 of the Snopes trilogy. Like *The Town,* it bears the subtitle "A Novel of the Snopes Family." Like *The Hamlet* and *The Town,* it is dedicated to Phil Stone.

Publication of *Faulkner in the University: Class Conferences at the University of Virginia, 1957–1958,* by the University Press of Virginia.[167]

1960   Faulkner continues to divide his time between Charlottesville and Oxford, where his mother lived until her death on 16 October at the age of 88. The Memphis *Commercial Appeal,* in her obituary notice, recalls her talents as a painter—she leaves nearly 600 paintings completed after 1941. Above all, however, she leaves "three sons, William of Charlottesville, John of Oxford, and Murry of Mobile, Alabama; four grandchildren, and eight great-grandchildren."

1961   *January*   Faulkner wills all his manuscripts to the William Faulkner Foundation. His daughter Jill is a member of the board.

Once more called upon for an official visit abroad, this time to Venezuela, Faulkner does not let himself be persuaded as easily as he was in 1954. On 17 January he writes: "I had hoped that the new administration by that time would have produced a foreign policy. Then amateurs like me (reluctant ones) would not need to be rushed to the front" (*SLWF,* p. 450).

16 February   Faulkner accepts an invitation from General William Westmoreland to visit the military academy at West Point.

8 [?] March   He asks Muna Lee of the State Department to "pass the word that I dont consider this [the trip to Venezuela] a pleasure trip, during which Faulkner is to be tenderly

---

[167] Reprinted by Random House as a Vintage Book in 1965.

shielded from tiredness and boredom and annoyance. That F. considers it a job, during which he will do his best to serve all ends which the N.A. [North American] Association aim or hope that his visit will do" (*SLWF*, p. 452).

2 April   Faulkner lands at Caracas. After a brief press conference, he goes to the home of his stepdaughter and her husband, William Fielden.

3 April   Another press conference in which Faulkner deftly handles embarrassing questions both on the foreign policy of the United States and on the racial issue. On the latter, "he did not hesitate to assign each race its specific responsibilities in searching for a solution."[168] He is the guest of President Rómulo Betancourt.

10 April   Faulkner leaves Venezuela.

Spring   *The Transatlantic Review* publishes Faulkner's homage to Albert Camus, which the *Nouvelle Revue française* published in French the year before in a special issue devoted to Camus after Camus' untimely death in 1960.[169] Faulkner authorized the publication in a letter dated 8 February 1960, in which he wrote: "I wrote it of course without any commercial thought at all: a private salute and farewell from one bloke to another doomed in the same anguish" (*SLWF*, p. 443).

11 June   The *New York Times* announces that the William Faulkner Foundation will encourage Latin-American writers and help promote the education of blacks in Mississippi.

2 August   Albert Erskine receives a letter from Oxford in which Faulkner announces that he has completed the first third of *The Reivers*. Somewhat prematurely, he requests him to consider the following statement for the jacket:

> An extremely important message . . . eminently qualified to become the Western World's bible of free will and private enterprise.
>
> > Ernest V. Trueblood
> > Literary & Dramatic Critic
> > Oxford, (Miss.) Eagle

---

[168] Quoted by Joseph Blotner, "William Faulkner, Roving Ambassador," p. 18.

[169] The French translation was published under the title "L'Ame qui s'interroge" in *Hommage à Albert Camus, 1913–1960* (Paris: Gallimard, 1967), pp. 143–44 (without the translator's name).

He thus goes back to the pseudonym he had used twenty-four years before.[170] And he adds: "Hot as hell here, as usual. Now it's 64 years I have said I'll never spend another summer in Miss." (*SLWF,* p. 455).

21 August In Oxford, Faulkner completes and dates the typescript of *The Reivers* (first entitled *The Horse-Stealers: A Reminiscence*), his last novel, in which he completes a project revealed twenty-one years ago in a letter to Robert Haas (see *3 May 1940*).

21 October Faulkner returns to Charlottesville.

27 November In New York with Albert Erskine, Faulkner revises *The Reivers* and goes back to work on the discrepancies in the Snopes trilogy.

Publication of James B. Meriwether's *The Literary Career of William Faulkner: A Bibliographical Study* by the Princeton University Library.

1962 *January* After another fall from a horse, Faulkner is hospitalized again. On 20 January, his uncle J. W. T. Falkner, Jr., dies.

23 March Faulkner is interviewed in Oxford for *The Cate Review* (*LITG,* pp. 270–81).

19 April Faulkner visits West Point with his wife, his daughter, and his son-in-law. A volume entitled *Faulkner at West Point* would be published in 1964, with the text of a passage from *The Reivers* which Faulkner read at West Point. This volume includes a collation of the spoken and the written versions.

20 April Faulkner declines an invitation from President John F. Kennedy to the White House.

6 May In Charlottesville, where he is considering moving from 917 Rugby Road to an expensive country house, Faulkner grants what is to be his last interview to Professor Vida Marković from the University of Belgrade (*LITG,* pp. 282–86).

24 May In New York, Eudora Welty presents to Faulkner the Gold Medal for Fiction awarded by the American Academy of Arts and Letters (*ESPL,* pp. 168–69).

---

[170] See *20–26 June 1937* and *mid-November 1943*.

4 June   Faulkner is in Oxford at the time of the publication of *The Reivers,* which is dedicated to "Victoria, Mark, Paul, William, Burks."[171]

6 July   At 1:30 A.M., Faulkner dies suddenly in Byhalia, Mississippi.[172] The death certificate gives the cause of death as "acute pulmonary edema" due "probably to a coronary thrombosis." His body is taken to Oxford where on 7 July, the burial takes place in the presense of about eighty persons, according to the Memphis *Commercial Appeal.* Among those present is novelist William Styron, who "covers" the event for *Life.* He will later publish his brief narrative under the title *As He Lay Dead, a Bitter Grief* (New York, 1981).

In his will, Faulkner named his daughter his sole literary executrix and willed his manuscripts to the William Faulkner Foundation. He left most of his possessions to his wife, $5,000 to his nephew James (John's son), and $5,000 to his niece, Mrs. Dean F. Mallard (Dean's daughter).

* * *

1962   Under the title of *William Faulkner: Early Prose and Poetry,* [*EPAP*], Carvel Collins publishes Faulkner's juvenilia, including several drawings.

1963   John Faulkner publishes his memoirs entitled *My Brother Bill: An Affectionate Reminiscence,* [*MBB*].
28 March   John Wesley Thompson Falkner III, William's second younger brother, dies.

1964   Publication of three books: the "unified" edition of the Snopes trilogy (New York: Random House); *William Faulkner's Library: A Catalogue,* [*WFLAC*] (comp. Joseph Blotner. Charlottesville: University Press of Virginia); and a collection of photographs by Martin Dain entitled *Faulkner's Country: Yoknapatawpha* (New York: Random House).

---

[171] The daughter of his stepdaughter, Mrs. Fielden, by her first marriage to Claude Selby; the son of his stepson, Malcolm Argyle Franklin; the three sons of his daughter Jill.
[172] See *31 January 1936.*

1965   Publication of *William Faulkner of Oxford* (Baton Rouge: Louisiana State University Press), a collection of memoirs and anecdotes by two professors at the University of Mississippi, James W. Webb and A. Wigfall Green.
9 October   Publication of "Mr. Acarius" (alternative title "Weekend Revisited") in *The Saturday Evening Post*, (pp. 26–31), and of *Essays, Speeches, and Public Letters*, [*ESPL*] (ed. James B. Meriwether. New York: Random House). Publication in a single volume of *The Marble Faun* and *A Green Bough* (New York: Random House).

1966   Publication of *The Faulkner-Cowley File: Letters and Memoirs, 1944–1962*, [*TFCF*] (New York: Viking Press).

1967   Phil Stone dies (see *Summer 1914*).
8 April   Publication of "The Wishing Tree" in *The Saturday Evening Post* (pp. 48ff.); this fairy tale was written by Faulkner in 1927 for the eighth birthday of Victoria Franklin who would become his stepdaughter. On 10 April, *The Wishing Tree* is published in book form (New York: Random House).
December   Publication of the memoirs of Murry C. Falkner, *The Falkners of Mississippi*, [*TFOM*] (Baton Rouge: Louisiana State University Press).

1968   *7 August*   Death of William Spratling (see *7 July 1925*). Publication of *Lion in the Garden: Interviews With William Faulkner, 1926–1962*, [LITG] (New York: Random House), a collection edited by James B. Meriwether and Michael Millgate. Also the publication of *William Faulkner: "Man Working," 1919–1962, A Catalogue of the William Faulkner Collections at the University of Virginia* (comp. Linton R. Massey. Charlottesville: University Press of Virginia).

1970   *31 August*   Discovery in "a broom closet under the staircase of Rowan Oak" of a box full of "nearly 1800 pages of handwritten working drafts and short stories" (see *5 August 1982*).

1971   Publication of Maurice Edgar Coindreau's prefaces and articles in *The Time of William Faulkner*, [*TTWF*] (Columbia: University of South Carolina Press).

1972   *7 January*   Mrs. Alabama McLean dies (see *7 May 1874*).
11 May   Lida Estelle Oldham Faulkner, widow of William Faulkner, dies.
Publication of John Bassett's *William Faulkner: An Annotated Checklist of Criticism* (New York: David Lewis).

1973   *22 August*   Publication of Douglas Day's edition of *Flags in the Dust* (New York: Random House), the original version of *Sartoris* (see *29 September 1927*).

1974   *March*   Publication of Joseph Blotner's *Faulkner: A Biography*, [*FAB*] (2 vols. New York: Random House).
August   First annual "Faulkner and Yoknapatawpha Conference" at the University of Mississippi.
Publication of *A Faulkner Miscellany*, [*AFM*], (ed. James B. Meriwether. Jackson: University Press of Mississippi).

1975   *Summer*   Publication of a limited edition in facsimile of the copy of *The Marionettes* (1920) (Charlottesville: Bibliographical Society of the University of Virginia), acquired by subscription in New York the preceding 27 February by the University of Virginia for $34,000.
October   Acquisition by two residents of Oxford of another copy of *The Marionettes* and publication of another limited edition (Oxford, Mississippi: Yoknapatawpha Press).
16 November   Opening of the exhibition at the University of Virginia's Alderman Library honoring Linton Reynolds Massey, 1900–1974: " 'Man Collecting': Manuscripts and Printed Works of William Faulkner at the University of Virginia Library." Publication by the University Printing Office of a limited edition of the catalogue bearing the same title.

1976   Publication of Meta Carpenter Wilde and Orin Borsten's *A Loving Gentleman: The Love Story of William Faulkner and Meta Carpenter* (New York: Simon and Schuster).

Publication of Thomas L. McHaney's *William Faulkner: A Reference Guide* (Boston: G. K. Hall).

Publication of a facsimile edition of *Mayday* (1926) (ed. Carvel Collins. Notre Dame, Indiana: University of Notre Dame Press).

1977 Publication of *Selected Letters of William Faulkner,* *[SLWF]* (ed. Joseph Blotner, New York: Random House).

1977 Publication of Malcolm Franklin's *Bitterweeds: Life With William Faulkner at Rowan Oak* (Irving, Texas: Society for the Study of Traditional Culture).

Publication of the trade edition of *The Marionettes* (ed. Noel Polk. Charlottesville: University Press of Virginia).

1979 Publication of the *Uncollected Stories of William Faulkner,* *[USWF]* (ed. Joseph Blotner. New York: Random House).

1980 Publication of *William Faulkner: A Life on Paper,* a transcription from the film produced by the Mississippi Center for Educational Television (Jackson: University Press of Mississippi).

March First International Faulkner Colloquium on "Faulkner and Idealism" organized by Michel Gresset and Patrick Samway, S.J., held at the Sorbonne and the Institut d'Anglais Charles V in Paris.

Publication of *Faulkner Studies: An Annual of Resarch, Criticism, and Reviews, No. 1* (ed. Barnett Guttenberg, Coral Gables: University of Miami Press). (This was the only volume published.)

1981 Publication of *Helen: A Courtship and Mississippi Poems,* *[HAC]* (introd. by Carvel Collins and Joseph Blotner (New Orleans and Oxford, Mississippi: Tulane University and Yoknapatawpha Press).

Publication of the first number of the *Faulkner Newsletter and Yoknapatawpha Review* (P.O. Box 248, Oxford, Miss. 38655).

Publication of *Sanctuary: The Original Text* (ed. Noel Polk. New York: Random House).

1982   *5 August*   Acquisition by the University of Mississippi of the "Rowan Oak Papers" (see *31 August 1970*).
Publication of *Faulkner's MGM Screenplays* (ed. Bruce F. Kawin. Knoxville: University of Tennessee Press).

1983   Publication of a limited edition of *Father Abraham* (1926–27) (ed. James B. Meriwether. New York: Red Ozier Press).
Publication of a limited edition of *A Sorority Pledge* (1933) (ed. Jane I. Haynes. Northport, Alabama: Seajay Press).
Publication of *Faulkner: A Comprehensive Guide to the Brodsky Collection, Volume I: The Biobibliography* (ed. Louis D. Brodsky and Robert W. Hamblin. Jackson: University Press of Mississippi).
December   Mr. and Mrs. Douglas Wynn donate forty-eight pages of Faulkner's poetry to the University of Mississippi; these pages were originally owned by Phil Stone.

1984   Publication of John Earl Bassett's *Faulkner: An Annotated Checklist of Recent Criticism* (Kent, Ohio: Kent State University Press).
Publication of *Vision in Spring* (1921) (ed. Judith Sensibar. Austin: University of Texas Press).
Publication of Joseph Blotner's *Faulkner: A Biography* ("one-volume edition, revised, updated, condensed") (New York: Random House).
June   First Faulkner meeting organized for Americans and Russians at the Gorky Institute in Moscow.
Publication of *Faulkner: A Comprehensive Guide to the Brodsky Collection, Volume II: The Letters* (ed. Louis D. Brodsky and Robert W. Hamblin. Jackson: University Press of Mississippi).
Publication of *Faulkner: A Comprehensive Guide to the Brodsky Collection, Volume III: The De Gaulle Story* (ed. Louis D. Brodsky and Robert W. Hamblin. Jackson; University Press of Mississippi.

1985   *April*   International Faulkner Conference organized by Japanese scholars in Izu, Japan.

Index